World's Oldest Fossils

Bruce L. Stinchcomb

4880 Lower Valley Road Atglen, Pennsylvania 19310

Other Schiffer Books on Related Subjects
Collecting Fluorescent Minerals, by Stuart Schneider
The World of Fluorescent Minerals, by Stuart Schneider

Designed by John P. Cheek
Cover deisgn by Bruce Waters
Type set in Bodoni Bd BT/New Baskerville BT

ISBN: 978-0-7643-2697-4
Printed in China

Published by Schiffer Publishing Ltd.
4880 Lower Valley Road
Atglen, PA 19310
Phone: (610) 593-1777; Fax: (610) 593-2002
E-mail: Info@schifferbooks.com

For the largest selection of fine reference books on this and related subjects, please visit our web site at **www.schifferbooks.com**
We are always looking for people to write books on new and related subjects. If you have an idea for a book please contact us at the above address.

This book may be purchased from the publisher.
Include $3.95 for shipping.
Please try your bookstore first.
You may write for a free catalog.

In Europe, Schiffer books are distributed by
Bushwood Books
6 Marksbury Ave.
Kew Gardens
Surrey TW9 4JF England
Phone: 44 (0) 20 8392-8585;
Fax: 44 (0) 20 8392-9876
E-mail: info@bushwoodbooks.co.uk
Website: www.bushwoodbooks.co.uk
Free postage in the U.K., Europe; air mail at cost.

Contents

Chapter One

Introduction

Fossils were puzzling to science well into the eighteenth century, and were variously considered as freaks of nature, as talismans placed into rocks by God to test one's religious beliefs, or as devices of the devil. Understanding of fossils and their meaning was often "muddy" in the science of the seventeenth and eighteenth centuries. The age of fossils and the rocks in which they were found were not significant issues in these centuries, as the age of the earth itself was still being debated by science. Scriptural considerations, such as the six days of Creation, were often taken literally and any really strong argument for a great age of the earth as modern geology, with its dependence upon megatime, was yet to appear.

Only a few years after Oliver Goldsmith's book was published, a Scotsman by the name of James Hutton published a work on geology in which long time intervals were a necessary pre-requisite to explain what he saw. Hutton's work was written in a very cumbersome style. (If you think these 1785 snippets from Goldsmith's work are hard going, try reading Hutton!)

The 1820s would see a more focused effort on understanding the workings of the earth through megatime, and by the late 1830s, the great age of the earth had become a scientific fact and modern geology was established. A succession of fossils found in the rock strata of Europe and the United States enabled the indexing of rock layers according to age. Such indexing of rock strata using fossils was the beginning of the geologic time scale. Early on, it was found that there was a thick sequence of strata that lacked fossils, which was always below strata that contained them. This "fossil free" strata was explained as representative of that part of earth history prior to the existence of life, while that strata containing the first fossils recorded the time when God created life. Such oldest strata bearing abundant and obvious fossils was to become known as the Cambrian system of strata, and the time when it was deposited as the Cambrian Period of geologic time.

The publication of Charles Darwin's *Origin of Species* prompted a closer look at these unfossiliferous layers to find supportive evidence for his theory, for if life had indeed evolved from very primitive forms the relatively advanced fossil life forms found in Cambrian strata were much too complex to be the earliest life; they had to have had more primitive ancestors. A search in these older rocks was minimally successful so that the sudden appearance of fossils in the Cambrian led Darwin to state:

> There is another...difficulty, which is much more serious. I allude to the manner in which species belonging to the main divisions of the animal kingdom suddenly appear in the lowest known fossiliferous rocks (those of the Cambrian Period). If the theory (evolutionary theory) be true, it is indisputable that before the lower Cambrian stratum was deposited, long periods elapsed...and that during these vast periods, the world swarmed with living creatures. As to the question why we do not find rich fossiliferous deposits belonging to these assumed earliest periods prior to the Cambrian, I can give no satisfactory answer. The case at present (1859) must remain inexplicable; and may be truly urged as a valid argument against the views here entertained.

C H A P. V.

Of Fossil-shells, and other extraneous Fossils.

WE may affirm of mr. Buffon, that which has been said of the chymists of old: though he may have failed in attaining his principal aim, of establishing a theory, yet he has brought together such a multitude of facts relative to the history of the earth, and the nature of its fossil productions, that curiosity finds ample compensation even while it feels the want of conviction.

Before, therefore, I enter upon the description of those parts of the earth, which seem more naturally to fall within the subject, it will not be improper to give a short history of those animal productions that are found in such quantities, either upon its surface, or at different depths below it. They demand our curiosity, and, indeed, there is nothing in natural history, that has afforded more scope for doubt, conjecture, and speculation. Whatever depths of the earth we examine, or at whatever distance within land we seek, we most commonly find a number of fossil-shells, which, being compared with others from the sea, or known kinds, are found to be exactly of a similar shape and

VOL. I. E

Fig. 01-01. Page from Oliver Goldsmith's 1785 *An History of the Earth and Animated Nature*, where he discusses fossils. In the second paragraph, Goldsmith writes: "They demand our curiosity and, indeed, there is nothing in natural history, that has afforded more scope for doubt, conjecture, and speculation." In the eighteenth century, the meaning and understanding of fossils was still muddy. (Note that an s looks like an f; this was characteristic of printed text until around 1806.)

---

34   A N   H I S T O R Y   O F

nature*. They are found at the very bottom of quarries and mines, in the most retired and inward parts of the most firm and solid rocks, upon the tops of even the highest hills and mountains, as well as in the vallies and plains: and this not in one country alone, but in all places where there is any digging for marble, chalk, or any other terrestrial matters, that are so compact as to fence off the external injuries of the air, and thus preserve these shells from decay.

These marine substances, so commonly diffused, and so generally to be met with, were, for a long time, considered by philosophers, as productions, not of the sea, but of the earth. "As we find that spars," said they, "always shoot into peculiar shapes, so these seeming snails, cockles, and muscle shells, are only sportive forms, that nature assumes among others of its mineral varieties: they have the shape of fish, indeed, but they have always been terrestrial substances†."

Fig. 01-02. A continuation of Goldsmith's fossil discussion after Buffon, a mid eighteenth century naturalist. Note that fpars = spars, crystalline minerals that usually fill cracks in rocks.

* In several parts of Asia and Africa, travellers have observed these shells in great abundance. In the mountains of Castravan, which lie above the city Barut, they quarry out a white stone, every part of which contains petrified fishes in great numbers, and of surprising diversity. They also seem to continue in such preservation, that their fins, scales, and all the minutest distinctions of their make, can be perfectly discerned‖.

Fig. 01-03. Discussion in Goldsmith's book of fossil fish from Beirut, Lebanon, where fossil fish in limestone slabs had been known for over two centuries but their organic origin at that time was still doubted by some.

Fig. 01-04. *Prionolepis* sp., a fossil fish from Upper Cretaceous rocks of Hajoula, Lebanon.

Fig. 01-05. Limestone slab with two fossil fish from the Cretaceous of Lebanon. Such well preserved fossils of obvious fish would seem hard to explain as a mineral phenomenon or freak of nature. (Value range F)

The first paleontologist to really seriously tackle the problem of the seeming absence of life from Precambrian rocks was Charles D. Walcott. Walcott had become interested in paleontology as a boy in upstate New York in the mid nineteenth century and was one of the first geologists to explore the Grand Canyon after it was floated by John Wesley Powell, the first head of the fledgling US Geological Survey. Powell, when meeting Walcott for the first time, liked his strong interest in fossils and offered him a position with the new survey. Walcott was sent to the canyon, penetrated into its inner gorge the best he could, and came up with a number of fossil-like objects, the most abundant of which are now known as stromatolites and which Walcott recognized as having some sort of biogenic origin.

One of the pitfalls Walcott and others would fall into was trying to relate these very old fossils with those produced in later times by more recent plants and animals. Walcott, for instance, thought that what are now known to be fragments of an algal mat were fragments of relatively highly evolved animals such as arthropods. Such "mistakes" were logical, as the Darwinian Theory presupposed a long, gradual evolutionary history prior to that of the relatively advanced animals found in Cambrian rock. In addition, the old adage of "hindsight is always easier than foresight" applies here—it's always easier to look backward and find errors made by a pioneer.

As one heads south from St. Louis, Missouri, into the Ozark Uplift, layer upon layer of sedimentary rock is exposed. Layers of strata that are thousands of feet below the surface under St. Louis come to the surface as you go southward, the younger layers having been removed by erosion with the more deeply buried layers taking their place. In many of these layers are found fossils, evidence of animals and plants that lived in ancient seas hundreds of millions of years ago. At a point about one hundred miles south of St. Louis, after going through more than a mile of ancient sediments exposed in the roadside cuts, strata is found which, unlike the layers above it, seem to lack fossils. At this point you have entered rock strata representative of that vast span of time called the Precambrian.

Fig. 01-06. Slice through a stromatolite of the type seen and collected from Precambrian rocks of the Grand Canyon by Charles D. Walcott.

Fig. 01-07. Specimen of *Cryptozoon*, or the "hidden animal." These were well-known fossils in the late nineteenth century but it remained a puzzle as to the type of organism they represented; some paleontologists suggested that they were giant rhizopods or foraminifera.

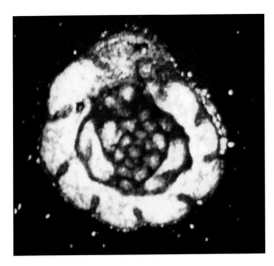

Fig. 01-08. A fossil foraminifera or "rhizopod." This is large for being the fossil of a single celled organism. Specimen from Permian strata of Japan. (Value range G)

Fig. 01-10. A single moneran mat "eurypterid fragment" up close. Deep Creek Canyon shale, Townsand, Montana.

Fig. 01-11. A fossil eurypterid *Eurypteris remipes*. Silurian, Bertie Formation, Williamsville, Ontario, Canada. (Value range F)

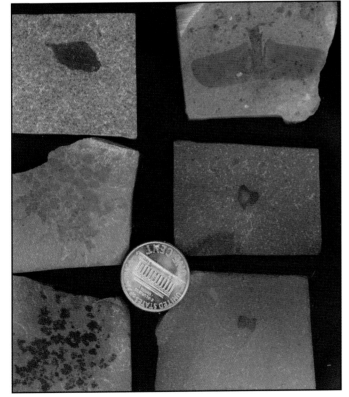

Fig. 01-09. Fragments of algal mats from mid-Precambrian age rocks that Charles Walcott thought were parts of eurypterids, a fairly complex arthropod. The specimen in the upper right is an actual eurypterid fragment.

Fig. 01-12. Primitive (inarticulate) brachiopods from the Cambrian sandstone at the "bottom of the stack" of Paleozoic sediments, Missouri Ozarks. Rock strata below the beds yielding these brachiopods lack obvious fossils and they are below the Cambrian strata, hence they are Precambrian. The phenomena of an absence of (obvious) fossils below beds carrying fossils like these Cambrian ones is a world wide phenomenon.

Precambrian rock strata is just that; it is **Pre-cambrian**—that is, it was formed before the Cambrian period of geologic time. The Cambrian Period is that part of earth history whose representative rock strata contains obvious fossils—fossils like trilobites and brachiopods as well as a variety of other types, usually invertebrates. In contrast, Precambrian rock strata seems to lack (obvious) fossils. This distinction was an early discovery of rock strata made in the British Isles during the 1820s and 30s, and has been found to be a worldwide phenomenon. Strata below that containing fossils was thought to be representative of a time in the history of the earth before there was life. In the last decades of the nineteenth century, peculiar structures in these "primordial" rocks were found that did look like fossils, but their biogenic origin couldn't be proven. They were given various names, and one name that took was stromatolite.

Stromatolites, the World's Oldest Fossils

Stromatolites represent the geologically earliest evidence of cells aggregating together to create a megascopic structure. Throughout earth history there has been a propensity for cells to aggregate, and stromatolites represent a manifestation of this organization. This propensity toward assembly and organization is reflected in the definition of a stromatolite, viz., a structure produced by the physiological activity of a **community** of microorganisms. Eukaryotic cells probably appeared in the mid-Proterozoic or possibly in the early Proterozoic if the fossil genus *Grypania* is considered to have been formed from eukaryotic cells. In a way, eukaryotic cells themselves represent a form of "cellular grouping" and can be looked at as a group of prokaryotic cells working together, "in committee." Such symbiotic grouping together of different prokaryotic cellular components is also one of the reasons for stromatolite diversity.

When one gets curious about fossils, a question that usually arises is "what are the oldest fossils?" Or, perhaps, "what are the earliest fossils known?"—depending upon how thoroughly a person thinks the earth has been geologically explored. "What are the oldest fossils" is not a trivial question, as fossils represent the tangible evidence for life that lived on the earth through vast spans of geologic time. The oldest fossils become a benchmark by which the question of "how long life has existed on the earth and what was it like?" can be placed on a factual basis. Fossils, representing the "hard data" (pun intended) on life of the geologic past have the potential for answering fundamental questions about life and its existence on earth—they are not trivial!

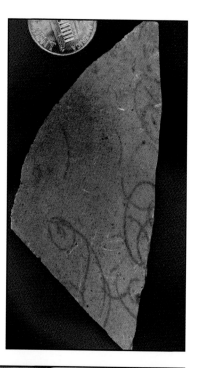

Fig. 01-13. These "curlicues" are impressions of *Grypania* sp., a 2.1 billion year old fossil from northern Michigan. It is one of the earliest candidates for the existence of eukaryotic celled organisms deep into the Precambrian. Early Proterozoic or Paleoproterozoic of Northern Michigan.

Fig. 01-14. One of many types of stromatolites. This stromatolite may have had eukaryotic cells as part of the microbial community that formed it. It is from the Phanerozoic Era and **not** from the Precambrian.

Pseudofossils and Dubiofossils

Nature can produce an endless variety of shapes (morphologies). Look at clouds for a while and sooner or later one will appear that is shaped like a rabbit, a donkey, or even a person's face. Rocks can do the same thing—look at enough of them and sooner or later you will find ones that resemble objects like cigars, fingers, beer steins, living animals, etc. Confusion once reigned over the explanation and meaning of fossils as late as the early nineteenth century. As noted earlier, sometimes fossils were considered to be freaks of nature, devices of the devil, or just shapes formed in rock layers that, like the cloud rabbits, happened to mimic distinct shapes. Those objects that resemble fossils but are **not,** are known as pseudofossils.

Even today, it is sometimes difficult to determine the difference between a true fossil and a pseudofossil.

Look at the supposed nannobacteria found in an SNC Martian meteorite in 1997. The same problem plagues identification of the world's earliest fossils. How do you determine whether a fossil-like object was really once part of something living or rather only looks like it was; the latter is a pseudofossil. If it is impossible to determine that a fossil-like object was once made by an organism, this object is known as a dubiofossil. Many early fossil-like objects fall into this category.

Some of the objects shown in this work are now considered pseudofossils, such as Eozoon; others are considered dubiofossils. Pseudofossil names are not shown in italics as they are not valid Linnaean names. However, when a Linnaean name is used in the context of the time frame of when the object was considered a fossil, its name is shown in italics.

Fig. 01-15. Pseudofossil-1, "Medusoids." Objects such as these have been confused with and considered to be fossil jellyfish (medusoids). The top ones in the photo are associated with geodes that formed this pseudofossil below where the geode "grew" in surrounding rock; the bottom pseudofossils are sections of concretions.

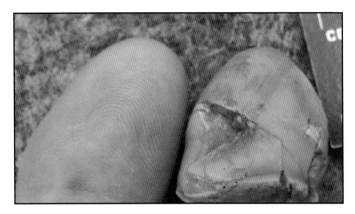

Fig. 01-16. Pseudofossil-2, "finger tip." Not only can pseudofossils resemble animals, they can resemble animal parts or organs as well.

Fig. 01-17. Pseudofossil-3, "Chrysanthemum stones." These are pseudofossils composed of radiating crystals. Such structures come in a wide variety of sizes and shapes, one clue that they are non-biogenic. Clusters of crystals such as these can easily be confused with the structures produced by primitive life forms. (Value range G)

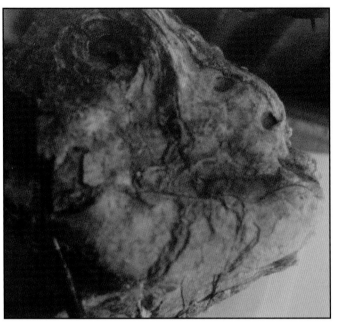

Fig. 01-19. Pseudofossil-5, "Reptile head." Concretions, particularly chert concretions, can take on a myriad of shapes like this "petrified dinosaur head."

Fig. 01-18. Pseudofossil-4, Denderites. Small crystals of manganese dioxide form these small fractual patterns to produce this common pseudofossil.

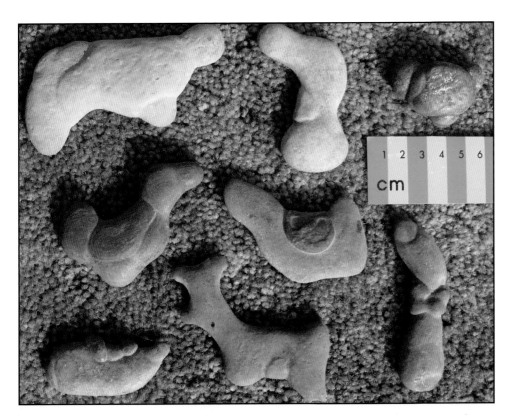

Fig. 01-20. "Crazy concretions." Glacial clays can contain concretions like these that can take on a variety of strange shapes. Some of them look like hot dogs, bow ties, and outlines of animals. They are almost comical pseudofossils. Glacial sediments, St. Croix River, eastern Minnesota. (Value range F, for group)

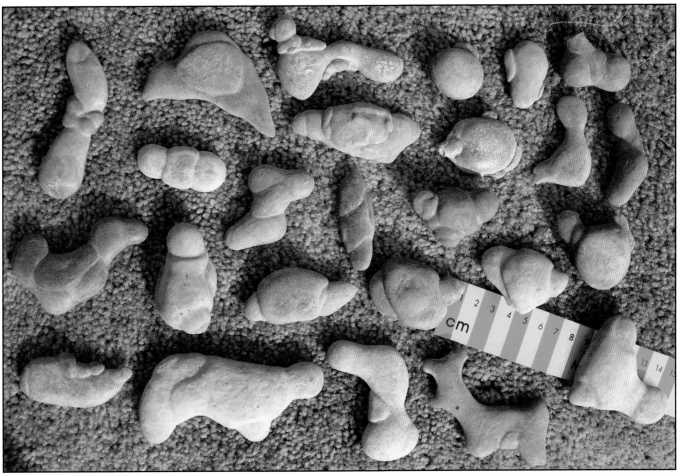

Fig. 01-21. Another group of concretions from glacial sediments with random shapes, many of which resemble animals. Pleistocene glacial sediments, St. Croix River, Minnesota. (Value range F, for group)

Literature on Early Fossils and Stromatolites

There is a sizeable collection of literature on stromatolites and related early fossils and pseudofossils, most of which is in the specialized literature of geology and paleontology. One of the purposes of this work is to visually present, in an appealing form, some of this diversity of early fossils. These objects, the earliest tangible remains of life, are not only scientifically significant, they can also be objects of exquisite beauty and are certainly collectible.

The literature on early life of the earth is predominantly found in technical publications of science, such as journals and bulletins. Such literature is generally housed in university or college libraries, and as a result much of it is not readily accessible to most persons—not only because of its location but also because of a "lack of knowledge" as to how to get into it to find a specific topic of interest. The Internet happily is allowing a level of access to some scientific information (and other information good and bad) that is unprecedented in its ease of accessibility. But even on the "net," technical terms and details can interfere with one's trying to access information such as that found here. (Try using **stromatolite** as a search word on the net.)

Fig. 01-22. Not only are fossils themselves collectible, the publications and literature on them are also collectible. Here is a collection of various nineteenth century US Geological Survey Monographs on fossils and geology published when the geology of western states and territories was initially being mapped and unraveled. (Value range E for individual book in good condition)

Fig. 01-23. Recent paleontological publications, including the *Journal of Paleontology* and the *Treatise on Invertebrate Paleontology* (at right). The *Journal of Paleontology* is one of the prime journals on paleontology in the world, with a focus on North American fossils. The *Treatise* is a definitive work attempting to cover all known fossils except vertebrates and plants.

Fossil enthusiasts, working with very ancient rocks of the Precambrian, viz., before the Cambrian, the age of the earliest strata yielding obvious fossils, occasionally ran into sedimentary rocks (usually limestone) containing reef-like structures as in the photo here. These appeared to be fossils, but unlike younger, bonafide ones, they seemed to lack a complex organic structure of bonafide fossils and because they occurred in such ancient rock strata (rock strata below that containing any undoubted fossils), many earth scientists refused to accept a biogenic origin for them.

Some of the most distinctive of these were digitate (finger-like) stromatolites, which occur in the mid-Precambrian Gunflint and Biwabik formations of the Lake Superior region of Canada and the United States. Examination of thin slices of these stromatolites in the early 1950s, under high optical magnification, led E. S. Barghoorn and Stanley Tyler to discover very tiny fossils associated with the stromatolites. This discovery opened the door for acceptance of other very ancient stromatolites as to their being of biogenic origin—hence pushing the occurrence of life deep into the early history of planet earth.

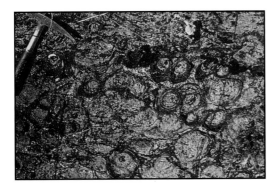

Fig. 01-24. Outcrop of a stromatolite reef. This glaciated surface of numerous stromatolites forming a reef is similar to the *Cryptozoon* reef of upstate New York, originally described in the late nineteenth century by James Hall.

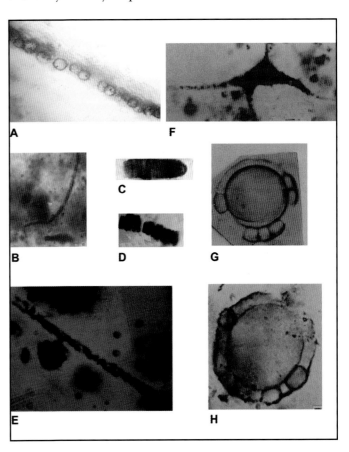

Fig. 01-25. Filament of cyanobacteria in Gunflint chert. It was microfossils like this that convinced geologists that Precambrian stromatolites really were of biogenic origin.

plicated by mats of microorganisms that build up on the sea floor. Monerans, particularly the cyanobacteria, can form such mats—abundantly so during the geologic past. Today such mats are relatively rare, as animals and protists crop them as food and they normally don't get a chance to develop extensively.

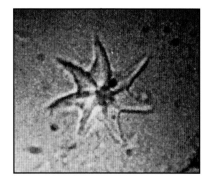

Fig. 02-04. Discoaster. Star-shaped fossil protists are attractive. These small protists seem to have appeared rather late in the history of life.

Through much of the Precambrian, however, such croppers were either absent or were rare, and moneran mats that formed remained un-molested. Sometimes these mats would be exposed to desiccation, such as during periods of low tide. As the mat desiccated, it would shrink, and sediment filled cracks between mat fragments would form patterns that resemble worm tracks. Other mat fragments rolled up or became bent, and impressions of these can resemble parts of animals. Such phenomena, in Precambrian rocks, have sometimes been mistaken for organisms and given Linnaean names.

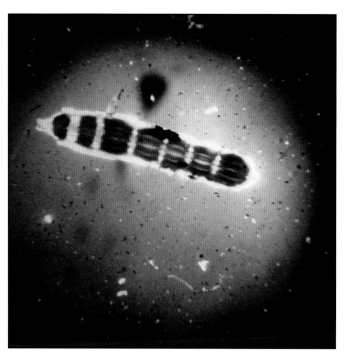

Fig. 02-07. *Nodosaria* sp. Another attractive fossil foram. Foraminifera are not only beautiful fossils, they also can be quite useful in indexing and determining the age of strata drilled in the process of petroleum exploration. Unlike most other fossils, which get ground up with the drill, forams can survive in drill cuttings so that the geological age of strata encountered by the drill can be determined.

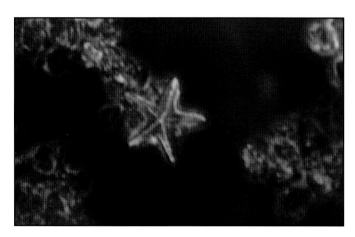

Fig. 02-05. Discoaster-2. Star-shaped fossils are interesting, however these microfossils are very small and geologically young.

Fig. 02-08. *Citharina* sp. Another attractive fossil foram, geologically young.

Fig. 02-06. *Gumbelina* sp. Snail-like test of a fossil foraminifera (foram). Foraminifera are single celled protists that have a protective test composed of calcium carbonate and can be common fossils but usually require a microscope to see. The earliest forams, like so many life forms, appear first in the Cambrian. Precambrian forams have been reported but they are probably in error. *Gumbelina* is the generic name in the Linnaean system; the sp. means species undetermined.

Fig. 02-09. Diatoms. These are single celled photosynthetic protists previously considered to be plants. Diatom fossils can compose beds of chalky strata called diatomaceous earth. Although they are primitive small life forms, they are relative late-comers in the history of life.

Geologic Time Scale

The geologic time scale is based upon fossils. The longest subdivisions of geologic time are called eras and there are five of them: the **Archean** (4.9 to 2.5 billion years b.p.), the **Proterozoic** (2.5 billion to 540 million years b.p.). the **Paleozoic** (540 million years to 235 million years b. p.), the **Mesozoic** (age of reptiles; 235 million to 67 million years b.p.) and the **Cenozoic** (67 million years to the present). The Archean and Proterozoic eras constitute the Precambrian part of geologic time.

The **Proterozoic** Era of the Precambrian is divided into three parts: the earliest part is called the **Paleoproterozoic**; the middle part, the **Mesoproterozoic**; and the youngest or third part the **Neoproterozoic**. This tripartite subdivision is used to mark the chapters of this book. The **Paleozoic** era is made up of seven subdivisions (periods), of which the Cambrian is the earliest. These periods (earliest to youngest) are **Cambrian, Ordovician, Silurian, Devonian, Mississippian, Pennsylvanian,** and **Permian**. Chapters Nine and Ten of the book deal with fossils of the Cambrian Period.

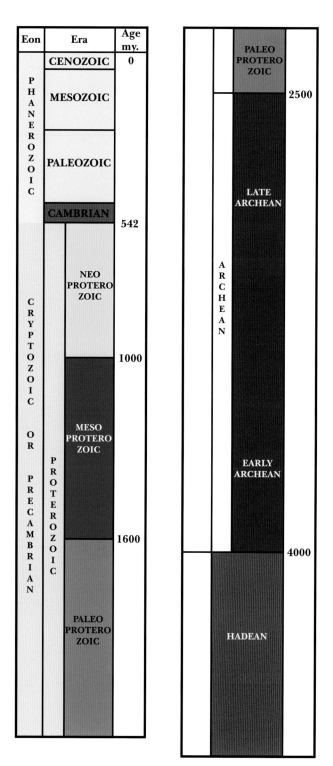

Fig. 02-10. The eras of the Precambrian. Pregeologic time is also known as the Hadean (see Chapter Four). The Hadean is that time **prior** to formation of geologic records on the earth, but well represented by the time period when most meteorites formed as well the cratered surfaces on the moon and Mars and the rock that composes these surfaces. The Archean is the most ancient part of the earth's geological record and the Proterozoic is the rest of the Precambrian before the Cambrian radiation event when fossils become relatively common. The Proterozoic is divided into three parts; the Paleoproterozoic (see Chapter Six), the Mesoproterozoic (Chapter Seven) and the Neoproterozoic (Chapter Eight). The Neoproterozoic is followed by the Cambrian Period of the Paleozoic Era.

Bibliography

Tsu-Ming Han and Bruce Runnegar, "Megascopic Eukaryotic Algae from the 2.1 Billion Year Old Negaunee Iron Formation." *Michigan Science,* 1992, Vol. 257, pp. 232-234.

Chapter Three

History and Discovery

Stromatoporoids and Stromatolites

The study of fossils (and consequently life of the geologic past) "took off" in Western Europe and North America during the third decade of the nineteenth century. This development was nothing less than the establishment of modern geology with its emphasis on geologic time, fossils, and strata. Among the more frequently found fossils in rock strata were corals and sponges. With such fossils, there was no question as to their biogenic origin as well as their position in the animal kingdom, as they had similar (but not exactly the same) anatomical features as those found in modern corals. These fossils often formed reef-like structures in strata that were also suggestive of the growth patterns of modern coral reefs. (Other fossils forming similar reef-like structures, were, however, not so easily identified with living organisms.)

These fossils were given the Linnaean name of *Stromatopora* and a number of different types were identified and named. Fossil Stromatopora (later called stromatoporoids), like fossil corals, gave no reason to question their biogenic origin as both exhibited complex, easily recognizable structures characteristic of living things.

Other puzzling fossil-like structures were found that occurred in reef-like patterns of growth like that of stromatoporoids, but that lacked the structural complexity seen in corals and stromatoporoids. These were compared to some primitive animals living in modern oceans and were given the suffix "zoon=g. zoo"(animal).

Fig. 03-01. Spherical stromatoporoid. These obviously organic structures were noted to be common fossils when fossils became a subject of serious scientific study in the early nineteenth century. Unlike stromatolites, similar looking stromatoporoids exhibit a fine regular structure easily recognizable as of biogenic origin. Distinct growth lines, similar to the growth lines of living organisms, also characterize stromatoporoids. Middle Ordovician, Central Tennessee. (Value range E)

Fig. 03-02. Slice through the same stromatoporoid as in previous photo, showing regular growth lines similar to those of a stromatolite.

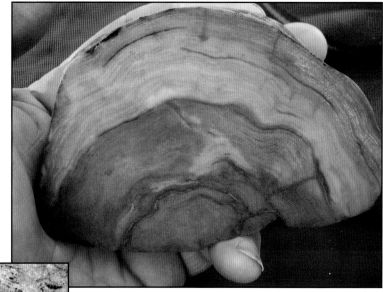

Fig. 03-03. Silicified stromatoporoid. This quartz replaced stromatoporoid was found as a glacial cobble. It could easily be mistaken for a stromatolite, except for the vertical dissepments faintly seen in this specimen. Middle Devonian, Iowa?, found as a glacial cobble transported to the St. Louis area during the (geologically recent) ice age. (Value range G)

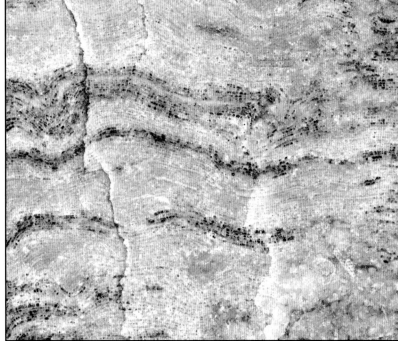

Fig. 03-04. *Stromatoporella tuberculata.* A slice through a stromatoporoid, clearly showing structural complexity (laminae and pillars) of a type not seen in stromatolites. Stromatoporoids, first described in 1826, have never been questioned as to their biogenic origin due to the presence of such structural complexity. As with stromatolites, the domes of stromatoporoids almost always point upward as a consequence of growth due to cell division. (Value range H)

Fig. 03-05. Rugose stromatoporoid. Stromatoporoids and stromatoporoid reefs became abundant in the Middle part of the Ordovician Period, some 455 million years ago. From this point until the end of the Paleozoic Era, they become part of ecosystems that overall lacked stromatolites. Prior to this time, however, stromatolites were very common in clear, shallow water environments where limestone formed. Stromatoporoids are a type of sponge, called a sclerosponge; they have survived to the present in very specialized environments. The rise of stromatoporoids, corals, and other reef-forming lower invertebrates was preceded by the termination of stromatolite dominated ecosystems at the end of the Lower Ordovician. Specimen from Middle Ordovician, Plattin Formation, Jefferson Co., Missouri. (Value range E)

One of the first of these recognized and described was *Cryptozoon*—literally, hidden animal. Others were *Archeozoon* from Canada (meaning ancient animal) and *Carelozoon* from Finland. The publication of Charles Darwin's *Origin of Species* in late 1859 gave impetus to finding the fossil records of some of the earth's earliest life. Darwin's evolutionary theory required a continuum of life going from very simple organisms grading gradually toward those of greater complexity. Creation, on the other hand—the concept taken by geologists prior to publication of the *Origin*—did not necessarily require such a continuum, as life forms within it were suddenly created by God.

In fact, the study of the fossil record up to this time seemed to support creation, as fossils appeared quite suddenly in rocks, seemingly without any ancestors, in strata called at the time the "Lower Silurian." Rock strata lower (and hence older) than that of the Lower Silurian (later to be called the "Cambrian Period"), seemed to lack fossils. Geologists looked for fossils in these older layers, but nothing seemed to be present.

Darwin's evolutionary theory provided motivation for a more thorough fossil search in these ancient rocks, for if it were true, Cambrian organisms had to have had ancestors and these should be found as fossils in the older, underlying layers. One of the more promising finds resulting from such intensified searches was groups of organic-like structures that seemed to form reefs like those of corals and stromatoporoids. Showing some structural complexity, these were found in beds of marble that crop out about 100 km north of Ottawa in the Province of Quebec, Canada. These fossil-like structures were given the Linnaean name of *Eozoon canadense*, or the "dawn animal of Canada,"

and were considered by many paleontologists at the time to have been earth's earliest life.

Eozoon was the first of a wide variety of "zoons" to be proposed, but by the beginning of the twentieth century, most paleontologists had come to the conclusion that it was not a once living organism but rather a pseudofossil (or false fossil). It is now considered as a pseudofossil; viz. an organic-looking mineral structure formed by metamorphism (change in rock through high pressure) and produced as a consequence of deep burial.

Early in the twentieth century, other puzzling structures, similar to *Cryptozoon*, came to the attention of paleontologists. Such structures, such as *Archeozoon*, were usually associated with limestones and were given, at this time, the general moniker of stromatoliths or stromatolites. What worried some geologists, however, was that many of these structures occurred in very ancient rock layers, **Pre**cambrian rock layers that otherwise seemed to lack fossils.

If the "zoons" found in such ancient rocks were indeed fossils, then life would have had to have existed much, much earlier than the Cambrian Period—the part of geologic time where fossils suddenly appear. Ambivalence prevailed, with some paleontologists refusing to recognize these structures as representative of ancient life, while others were really intrigued with them because of the great antiquity of the strata that yielded them, and so focused on studying them.

One of the latter was Charles D. Walcott of the U.S. Geological Survey and the Smithsonian Institution. Walcott, best known as the discoverer of the unique fossils of the Cambrian Burgess shale, systematically investigated reports of stromatolites

Fig. 03-06. Plan view (top view) of Cryptozoon *proliferium* Hall. The Linnaean name, *Cryptozoon proliferium* ("prolific hidden animal"), was given to enigmatic concentric structures like these by James Hall in 1888. These were found to form reef-like masses in dolomite outcrops near Saratoga Springs, New York. Other occurrences were discovered in similar age rocks in Virginia, Georgia, and Alabama, and—as with the New York occurrence—were attributed to being formed by gigantic protozoans (now protists). In 1907, fossils such as these were considered by Charles Walcott and others to be a type of trace fossil made by blue-green algae and were given the general name of stromatolith. Stromatoliths or stromatolites like these, besides being found in Proterozoic rocks, are particularly common in strata of the Cambrian and earliest third of the Ordovician Period; after that time they are much less frequently seen. Upper Cambrian, Southern Missouri. (Value range F)

and other fossil-like objects found in these very ancient rocks. Walcott did much of his work near the end of the nineteenth and early in the twentieth century, when the geology of the western parts of the United States and Canada was being unraveled. He investigated very ancient rocks of western Ontario as well as other parts of the ancient Canadian Shield, but his focus was primarily on less deformed and less metamorphosed strata of the western mountain ranges, such as the Belt Supergroup of Montana, Idaho, and British Columbia. In these rocks, Walcott discovered and described a suite of puzzling, fossil-like structures, many of which are still controversial today.

After Walcott's work, interest in stromatolites muddled along, and more and different types continued to turn up. Stromatolites in younger rock strata didn't cause much concern, however it was those found in the very ancient rocks of the Precambrian that still worried and puzzled geologists and paleontologists. Because of the great age of many of these occurrences, there was still a strong inclination to consider stromatolites as pseudofossils, for if indeed they were biogenic it would mean that life was on the earth for much of its existence. Such a long existence seemed to run contrary with the sudden appearance of obvious fossils some 550 million years ago at the beginning of the Cambrian Period.

Fig. 03-07. While *Cryptozoon* occurs most commonly in Cambrian and Lower Ordovician limestones, cherts, and dolomites (strata of the Paleozoic Era), it can also occur in much more ancient strata as well. This is one of the reasons why many geologists doubted *Cryptozoons*' biogenic interpretation. This specimen is from a Paleoproterozoic limestone some 2.3 billion years old. Medicine Bow Mts., Wyoming. (Value range G)

Fig. 03-08. This *Cryptozoon* reef in the Missouri Ozarks was attributed to some sort of lower invertebrate "animal." In the mid-twentieth century, its algal origin was acknowledged and recognized as a type of stromatolite.

Fig. 03-09. Stromatolites such as this were described and illustrated in many geologic reports during the first six decades of the twentieth century. Most were from strata of the Cambrian or the first third of the Ordovician Period (Lower Ordovician). Many geologic reports of the 1940s and 50s in Alabama, Georgia, New Jersey, and Missouri make reference to them. By this time, such structures in Phanerozoic rocks were usually attributed to the physiological activity of blue-green algae (or what are now called cyanobacteria).

Fig. 03-10. *Archeozoon acadiense.* One of the "zoons" (or "zoans") found and described in the late nineteenth century, these "most ancient animals of Acadia" were, like Eozoon, first considered as gigantic protozoans or protists. Their algal origin was later suggested by Charles D. Walcott. Greenhead Group, Greenhead Peninsula near St. John, New Brunswick, Canada. (Value range F)

Fig. 03-11. *Archaeozoon acadiense* Matthew. This is part of a large mass of Archaeozoon, a distinctive Proterozoic stromatolite that was one of the first described from the Precambrian.

Fig. 03-12. Large domal stromatolites in dipping or tilted strata of Permian age south of Casper, Wyoming.

Below:
Fig. 03-15. These are large fossil Protozoans of the genus Nummulites. *Cryptozoon* was envisioned as a variant on these where the protozoan (or protists) merged into each other. The generic name refers to the coin-like shape of the fossil, viz. numismatics. These fossils were well-known in the paleontology of the nineteenth century, as limestone used to build the Egyptian pyramids is full of them. (Value range H)

Fig. 03-13. This glaciated surface of a stromatolite reef is similar to the Cambrian age *Cryptozoon* reefs in northern New York state, which were first described by James Hall in 1888. Those shown here are from Paleoproterozoic strata of northern Quebec, so that they are much older than the Cambrian *Cryptozoon* of New York state.

Fig. 03-14. Side view of a weathered surface of a *Cryptozoon* specimen. Cambrian of Missouri. (Value range G)

Fig. 03-16. Transverse slice through a stromatolite dome. Concentric pattern through such a dome represents the various layers of monerans that grew to form the stromatolite. Oneota Formation, Southeastern Minnesota. (Value range F)

Fig. 03-17. *Eozoon canadense,* the "dawn animal of Canada," was one of the first Precambrian "fossils" to be described. Its discovery in 1865 was a consequence of efforts to more extensively explore very ancient (Precambrian) strata. This search for fossils in such ancient strata was promulgated by the publication of Charles Darwin's *Origin of Species* in late 1859. A quest for finding the ancestors of Cambrian fossils like trilobites, sponges, etc. intensified after publication of the *Origin,* as evolution—unlike creation—necessitated the existence of such ancestors. This slice through an *Eozoon* "colony" is wrapped around an elongated diopside nodule. *Eozoon* today is considered as a pseudofossil, however, its structure in part may have been inherited from a group of stromatolites now metamorphosed beyond recognition. From the Cote St. Pierre locality about 100 km north of Ottawa, Ontario.

Fig. 03-18. *Archaeospherina* is the generic name given for these concretionary spherules found in association with *Eozoon canadense.* They were considered by advocates of the biogenicity of *Eozoon* to be the reproductive "buds" or clones of the *Eozoon* "animal." These spherical "buds," like other portions of *Eozoon,* are composed of serpentine, a mineral rarely associated with fossils. Laurentian (Grenville) Mesoproterozoic marble, Cote St. Pierre locality, Quebec.

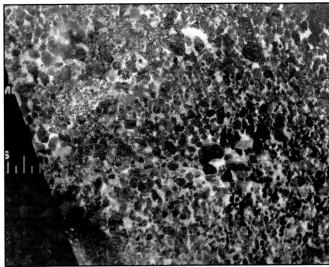

Fig. 03-19. Weathered surface of Eozoon. In outcrop, this pattern is developed on the weathered surfaces of Eozoon. It resembles the pattern seen on weathered surfaces of fossils such as foraminifera or what was known at the time of the Eozoon controversy as a rhizopod. (Value range E)

Fig. 03-20. Slice through mass of Eozoon. The white band is a crack along which internal weathering has occurred. From Cote St. Pierre locality, Quebec.

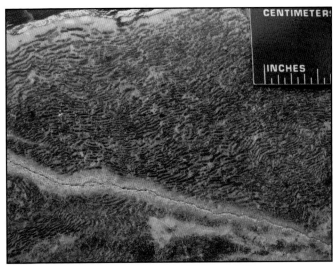

The situation changed in 1965, when paleontologist Elso S. Barghoorn reported microscopic fossils associated with quite ancient stromatolites of the Precambrian Gunflint Formation. These small fossils were preserved in a manner somewhat similar to that by which insects are preserved in amber, but sealed in silica (quartz). They were associated with stromatolites in a sequence of strata cropping out in the Lake Superior Region of the Canadian Shield. The Gunflint chert contains beds of BIF or banded iron formation, which across the border in Minnesota makes up iron-rich strata that form the iron ore deposits of that state. This rock unit also carries contains many stromatolites. The occurrence of these exquisitely preserved microfossils in stromatolites led most paleontologists to accept the organic origin or biogenicity of stromatolites, regardless of how ancient the strata in which they were found.

Recognition by some that the growth and physiological activity of primitive photosynthetic life, the blue-green algae (now called cyanobacteria), was responsible for the creation of stromatolites took place in the early part of the twentieth century but was ignored by many paleontologists as it couldn't be proven. Further investigations on the cell structure of cyanobacteria and distinctions in its cell structure from that of the cells of other types of life emphasized the distinctiveness and primitive nature of the blue-green algae cell. (This type of cell is called prokaryotic.)

Compared to the structure of the eukaryotic cell (the cell type found in animals and plants), that of the prokaryotic cell type is much simpler and more primitive. This relative simplicity of the cells of prokaryotes was in agreement with their occurrence going much, much further back in geologic time than do representatives of the other four kingdoms of living things: animals, plants, protists, and fungi. The fact that stromatolites are found in some of the earth's oldest rock layers forms the basis for the statement that "life has been on the earth for at least 3.5 billion years," which is the age of these oldest known stromatolites.

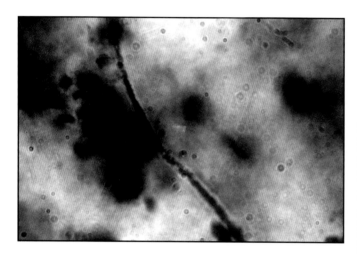

Fig. 03-21. Cyanobacterial filament from the Gunflint chert. Microfossils such as this convinced skeptical earth scientists that very ancient stromatolites such as those of the Gunflint Formation were really biogenic.

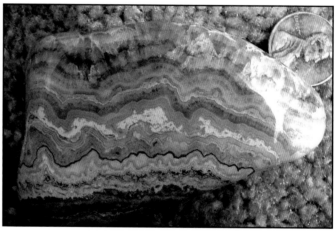

Fig. 03-23. Non biogenic banding. Various phenomena can produce banding which might be mistaken for that produced in a stromatolite, such as seen in this banded agate. Stromatolitic banding has a distinct signature that is usually recognizable to a person familiar with stromatolites; the pattern here is **not** that signature.

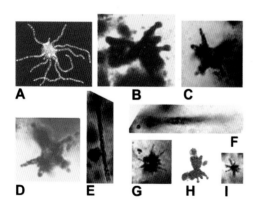

Fig. 03-22. Small organisms found in abundance in the 2.1 billion year old Gunflint chert. These small fossils were responsible for forming the Gunflint as well as other Paleoproterozoic stromatolites. The occurrence of these also convinced scientists that Precambrian stromatolites were indeed biogenic, and that life is a very ancient phenomena on the earth.

Eozoon and Pseudofossils

Eozoon canadense, when observed in outcrop on a rocky hillside, seems to form reef-like masses lying upon masses of diopside, a high temperature silicate mineral. Eozoon itself is composed of calcite, serpentine, and epidote, the latter two silicate minerals not commonly associated with fossils. This minerals' incongruity was pointed out by the critics of Eozoons' biogenicity. It is often quite difficult to distinguish a group of crystals that have grown together in clusters from forms taken by a group of primitive animals such as sponges, corals, fungi, or other radially symmetrical organisms that have also grown together, in clusters like crystals. This is particularly true if the rocks containing such structures have been changed or metamorphosed as a consequence of pressure, as is the case with most very ancient sedimentary rocks.

Sometimes pseudofossils found in ancient rocks look as organic as do associated stromatolites. Such confusion is exemplified by another discovery made by C. D. Walcott, given the generic name of *Atikokania* sp. This "fossil" occurs in an Archean black limestone and iron formation sequence in northwestern Ontario. Walcott considered *Atikokania* to be a very early example of an archeocyathid. Archeocyathids themselves are puzzling fossils, occurring as part of the earliest Cambrian faunas and seemingly, like other Cambrian fossils, having no known Precambrian ancestors. Originally thought to be a sort of extinct sponge, the taxonomic position of archeocyathids has always been questionable but the biogenicity of archeocyathids has never been questioned. Archeocyathids have attributes of both sponges and corals but their sponge designation is weak, as they lack a diagnostic feature of sponges, the presence of spicules. Walcott's placement of *Atikokania* as a very early ancestor of archeocyathids seemed as reasonable a placement as any, and there it remained, in limbo, for six decades. Late twentieth century re-interest in very early fossils re-evaluated it and, like *Eozoon,* it is now considered a pseudofossil formed as a consequence of crystal growth—but crystal growth that occurred in association with growth of unquestioned stromatolites. This confusion of crystals and crystal clusters with bonafide fossils surfaced more recently with the problem of the organized elements of meteorites and again in the early part of this century with of tiny elongate, fossil-like structures called "nannobacteria," which occur in a lime-filled crack in the Allen Hills meteorite, a rock blasted by impact from the surface of Mars.

Fig. 03-24. Outcrop of black, carbonaceous certified stromatolites in the Gunflint Formation, Nolalu, northwestern Ontario.

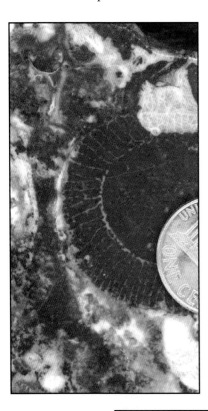

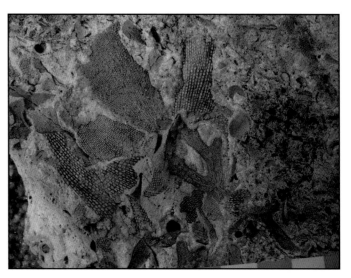

Fig. 03-25. A group of archeocyathids from Lower Cambrian rocks of Labrador. Archeocyathids are puzzling Cambrian fossils. *Atikokania*, a pseudofossil found in the Archean, was considered to be a very early and primitive archeocyathid.

Fig. 03-26. Another archeocyathid, these small forms are from Lower Cambrian marble in what were originally thought to be Precambrian rocks before archeocyathids were found in them.

Fig. 03-27. Lacy bryozoans. Another "zoan," but in this case one that appears after the Cambrian period and is still living. They were abundant colonial marine animals starting in the Middle Ordovician, and are still abundant in shallow water of seas today, although modern bryozoans are usually not conspicuous.

Fig. 03-28. A stromatoporoid and *Cryptophragmus* sp., an elongate fossil thought to be a type of stromatoporoid. These puzzling fossils are probably peculiar sponges. Plattin Limestone, Jefferson County, Missouri (Value range F)

Moneran Mats and Stromatolites

A variety of puzzling structures have been described as fossil burrows in Precambrian rocks. If these were bonafide burrows, their great age would mean that animals appeared very early in earth's history, much earlier than the Cambrian Period when the animal fossil record "becomes clear." What has become clear with the Precambrian fossil record, is that throughout most of this long time span bacteria and cyanobacteria were the dominant or perhaps the only forms of life on earth. The prokaryotic life forms of the Kingdom Monera would occupy favorable environments in shallow water where they would produce mats of bacteria or cyanobacteria. Such moneran mats, when broken up by storms or when exposed to drying and shrinking, would produce fragments. Sometimes these fragments curl up and these have been confused with trace fossils made by animals. Most of the Pre-Neoproterozoic tracks, burrows, and other "trace fossils" can be explained as mat fragments produced in some way from parts of moneran mats. Moneran mats really dominate the Precambrian fossil record, as laminar stromatolites are themselves really layers of moneran mats, and stromatolite domes and fingers can be considered as types of "sculpted" moneran mats.

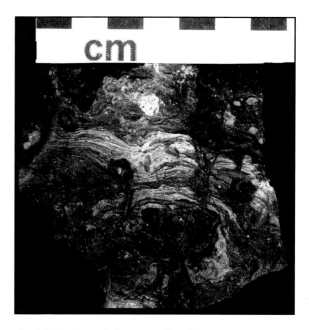

Fig. 03-30. Group of stromatolite-like structures in volcanic ash similar to previous photo, now lithified to a rock called tuff.

Fig. 03-29. Domal stromatolite? Preserved in volcanic ash (tuff). Stromatolites are usually found in limestone or chert, but they can be formed in other environments as well. The sticky mucilage of cyanobacteria can accumulate and bind particles of sediment such as the fine ash particles that compose this structure. The stromatolitic signature shown here however, is unclear. These structures may have been formed by growth of moneran mats in shallow, volcanically formed lakes; their origin is unclear. Rock Pile Mountain near Fredericktown, Missouri.

Fig. 03-31. Slab with *Collenia undosa*, Gunflint Formation, Paleoproterozoic. Most of the stromatolites from the Biwabik and Gunflint Formations are labeled as *Collenia undosa* by collectors and fossil dealers. In fact, there are a number of stromatolite form genera in these strata, often with one form grading into another. *Kussiella* sp. forms straight "fingers" similar to this but does not bifurcate. Nolalu, Northwestern Ontario, Canada.

Fig. 03-32. Weathered surface of a stromatoporoid. Such fossils can easily be confused with a stromatolite, however the difference can be determined by the presence of dissepiments in a stromatoporoid, which will be absent in a stromatolite. Devonian, Southwestern Virginia. (Value range F)

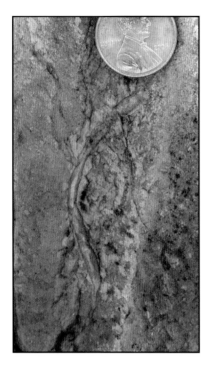

Fig. 03-33. Pseudofossils like this "worm track" are formed from sediment filling shrinkage cracks developed in a moneran mat. Often these have been confused, when found in Precambrian rocks, with worm tracks. If they *were* worm tracks, it would put motile life forms, which are all presumably animals, far back into the Precambrian.

Fig. 03-34. These are desiccation cracks formed from the shrinkage of a moneran mat (probably cyanobacteria). Fragments of such mats can form patterns that resemble animal fossils.

Bibliography

Awramik, S. M. "Gunflint stromatolites; Microfossil distribution in relation to stromatolite morphology." In M. R. Walter, ed. *Stromatolites*, Elsevier, Amsterdam, 1976.

Barghoorn, E. S. and Stanley A. Tyler. "Microorganisms from the Gunflint Chert." *Science* Vol. 147, No. 3658, 1965, p. 563-577.

Cloud, Preston E., Jr. "Significance of the Gunflint (Precambrian) Microflora." *Science*, Vol. 143, No. 366. 6 p., 1965.

Day, William. *Genesis on Planet Earth; The Search for Life's Beginning*. Yale University Press, 1984.

Gould, Stephen J. "An Early Start," in *The Panda's Thumb*. W. W. Norton Co., New York and London. 1980.

Gould, Stephen J. "Bathybius and Eozoon," in *The Panda's Thumb*. W. W. Norton Co., New York and London. 1980.

Gould, Stephen J. "Crazy old Randolph Kirkpatrick," in *The Panda's Thumb*. W. W. Norton Co. New York and London. 1980.

LaBerge, Gene L. "Microfossils and Precambrian Iron-Formations." *Bulletin of the Geological Society of America*. Vol. 78, 1967, p. 331-342.

Tyler, Stanley A., and Elso S. Barghoorn. "Occurrence of Structurally Preserved Plants in Pre-Cambrian Rocks of the Canadian Shield." *Science*, Vol. 119, No. 3096, 1954, p. 606-608.

Yochelson, Ellis L. *Charles Doolittle Walcott – Paleontologist*. Kent, Ohio and London, England: The Kent State University Press, 1998.

Yochelson, Ellis L. *Smithsonian Institution Secretary, Charles Doolittle Walcott*. Kent, Ohio and London, England: The Kent State University Press, 2001.

Chapter Four
The Hadean and the Carbonaceous Chondrites

That part of geologic time before the oldest known earth rocks were formed (that is before the Archean Era) is called the Hadean. It was during this time that the earth was bombarded with asteroids and meteorites, producing large numbers of craters, and had a lava-like (mafic) crust that was partially molten (magma ocean). Few earthly geologic records exist from this time; its occurrence on the earth is inferred from records of the other planets of the inner Solar System. Besides meteorites and moon rocks, Hadean records consist of original planetary surfaces scarred with a large number of craters such as those seen on the Moon, of which most were formed during the first 500 million years of these planets' existence. The earth had to have had similar cratering, however later geologic processes erased this earliest of earthly records but preserved it on Mercury, the Moon (Luna), and parts of Mars (the extensively cratered part of the Martian southern hemisphere).

The oldest rocks, being the oldest unmodified things you can hold in your hand, are meteorites. Some meteorites or parts of meteorites predate the formation of the Solar System and have been dated by geochronological methods at over 6 billion years old. The topic of meteorites is potentially an involved one, but suffice it to say that meteorites are rocks, and rocks, being solids, can preserve information, including that of the possible presence of life where they were formed. A group of meteorites known as the carbonaceous chondrites have attributes that make them a suitable topic for a work on early fossils. This attribute is the presence of organic compounds, compounds such as hydrocarbons, amino acids, aldehydes and others, which are usually found associated with life and for which reason are called organic compounds.

Even in consideration of the above, the inclusion of carbonaceous meteorites (which are not fossils) in a work on fossils might appear incongruous to some in light of the fact that a very profound distinction exists between organic compounds in meteorites and earthly fossils. This distinction is of course, the distinction between the living and the non-living. Advocates for a continuum of evolution de-emphasize the magnitude of the gap between simple organic molecules, such as those in the carbonaceous chondrites, and the very complex molecules such as RNA, DNA, proteins, or even chlorophyll, which characterize life. Stromatolites and other fossils are (or were) made by living things, and they were once part of the biosphere; simple organic molecules were not necessarily part of any biosphere. Simple organic molecules like those of the carbonaceous chondrites are believed by most scientists, however, to have been the raw materials which, through chemical evolution, led to the first primitive living things, presumably some sort of archeria or bacteria.

Evolution of organisms over megatime is a fact, and the various types of life on the earth form such a continuum—a continuum going from bacteria to man. It has been stated that the entire field of biology makes sense only in light of evolution. Natural selection, the major mechanism of evolution, is able to explain many if not most phenomena found in the biosphere. Chemical evolution, that is, going from the non-living to the living, is another matter. Although chemical pathways have been proposed as to how chemical evolution might have happened, nothing in the fossil or rock record (or, for that matter, in the biochemistry of living cells) really throws any light on the matter.

The Carbonaceous Chondrites

The amino acids and other organic compounds found in a group of meteorites known as the carbonaceous meteorites are simple molecules, many of which are the "building blocks" of living things. Similar compounds have been produced abiogenically in the laboratory by the famous "Miller Experiment," first done in the early 1950s, but such compounds are a far cry from being living! A vast gap exists between these simple molecules and those such as DNA, RNA, or proteins, the complex molecules that characterize living things. Chemical evolution has been inferred as the mechanism that allowed such simple molecules to join together in just the right combination, forming a self-catalyzing molecule which could then reproduce itself. This, with additional combinations, led to a self-reproducing proto-cell and eventually to life. Chemical pathways as to how this all might have happened have been suggested, but they have little more support than does the nifty statement by Charles Darwin at the conclusion of the *Origin*: "I can imagine some warm, little pond teeming with ammoniacal salts acting together to produce results which led to the primordial form of life." The step from non-living to living matter is the most profound obstacle to be crossed using the explanation of evolution as the mechanism responsible for life.

Carbonaceous chondrites were first recognized in the mid-nineteenth century, when one fell and was recovered shortly after it fell, then chemically analyzed. Analysis of the black matrix between the chondrules showed, to the surprise of scientists of the time, the presence of organic compounds. The predominant compounds detected were high molecular weight hydrocarbons, compounds similar to those found in asphalt and from which chemical category was derived the name carbonaceous meteorites. Interest in the carbonaceous chondrites revived in the 1950s when additional specimens fell to earth, coupled with the availability of superior analytical techniques that enabled a more sophisticated chemical analysis. These superior techniques revealed not only hydrocarbons, but also ring or aromatic hydrocarbons, amino acids, aldehydes, alcohols, and porphyrins, all compounds usually associated with living things. For various reasons these "organic" compounds are believed to be of an inorganic or an abiogenic origin, produced akin to the compounds formed in the Miller Experiment. Since they form part of the matrix material between chondrules in the meteorite, they must have been produced in the nebula responsible for the formation of such material. Matter that forms this matrix between chondrules was the matter given off by novas and red giant stars and interacted in a nebula.

Organized Elements

In carbonaceous chondrites are found in the meteorite's matrix the "organized elements." The Orgueil carbonaceous chondrite, which fell in France in 1863, and a similar one, which fell near Murray, Kentucky in 1951, were two of a number of carbonaceous chondrites analyzed for organic compounds. Examination of thin sections of these meteorites under high magnification revealed small, fossil-like structures that resembled steering wheels or peace symbols. These minute structures, given the non-committal name of organized elements, were suggested by some scientists at the time to be fossils. The implications of this, that the organized elements were really fossils, is obvious. This extraterrestrial fossil idea was quickly replaced by a less extraordinary one, holding that the organized elements were small crystals—small crystals that had formed in a zero gravity environment similar to that which produced the spherical chondrules and under conditions somewhat analogous to that which can form snow flakes.

A similar scenario surfaced thirty-five years later, with the discovery of bacterial-like dubiofossils in a Martian meteorite (SNC) from the Antarctic. Like false alarms in the earthly fossil record as with *Eozoon*, after a period of discussion in science, such extraordinary claims are generally abandoned. (Extraordinary claims in science require extraordinary verification.) The organized elements in meteorites appear to be part of the synthesis process that produced the organic compounds in the meteorites themselves and relate to a seemingly commonplace phenomena in deep space.

The reddish, hydrocarbon haze on Titan (a satellite of Saturn) and the brownish "goo" in the upper atmosphere of Jupiter appear to be products of the inorganic synthesis of organic compounds. In terms of simple organic compounds such as amino acids, alcohols, and aldehydes, there doesn't appear to be a distinction between compounds made by abiotic processes and those made by biotic ones. On the other hand, the complex molecules of DNA, proteins, etc. sets the earth's biosphere into a class by itself, a unique category of matter, the origin of which is at present is totally unknown to science.

Fig. 04-01. Cold Bokkeveld meteorite. Fragment of a famous carbonaceous chondrite that fell in the mid-nineteenth century. Small silicate chondrules are set in a matrix containing carbonaceous material like that of the Murchison meteorite (see next page). Nineteenth century analytical techniques showed the presence of organic compounds in this and other similar meteorites, but they were suspected as being from terrestrial contamination.

Fig. 04-02. In January 2000, an atmospheric fireball accompanied by sonic booms (bolide) preceded the landing of a 39+ gram carbonaceous chondrite, a piece of which landed in the snow cover of frozen Tagish Lake, British Columbia, Canada, and was recovered shortly thereafter. Like most carbonaceous chondrites, this specimen is very friable as well as combustible with the friction generated upon entry into the earth's atmosphere. Placement of a small piece of this meteorite on a flatbed scanner, even with support, caused the fragment to crumble as seen here. White objects are small high temperature (pyroxene) silicate bodies. Specimen is 4 mm across. (Value range G)

Fig. 04-03. Murray, Kentucky (CM2 carbonaceous chondrite). A fireball over western Kentucky heralded the arrival of this carbonaceous chondrite in 1951. As with other CM2 meteorites, the black matrix is rich in organic compounds, primarily asphaltic or tar-like material. The white objects are silicate chondrules, which formed from material produced in a nebula prior to the formation of the solar system. Examination in the 1960s of thin sections of Murray revealed very small steering wheel or peace symbol-like structures referred to as organized elements. Similarly, such "organized elements" were found in the first carbonaceous chondritic meteorite to have been recognized, Orgueil, which fell in France in the mid-nineteenth century. At the time of their discovery, organized elements were thought by some workers to be small fossils (microfossils). Like the nannobacteria of the Allen Hills meteorite, organized elements are considered to be a "false alarm" regarding the fossil existence of extraterrestrial life. Millimeter scale at bottom. (Value range D)

Fig. 04-04. Warrenton, Missouri, fall January 1877. A small carbonaceous chondrite was recovered after a brilliant fireball was seen over Missouri in 1877. A piece of this meteorite was recovered near Warrenton, Missouri, northwest of St. Louis and now along I-70. Like most other carbonaceous chondrites, this specimen is very friable and delicate. Most carbonaceous meteorites burn up upon entrance into the earth's upper atmosphere. It helps if the meteorite enters the earth's atmosphere in the same direction as the earth is traveling around the sun, so that the velocity of entry is lower, which gives less friction. This lower velocity of entry prevents total destruction of the meteorite by ablation and combustion. Dark areas are concentrations of carbonaceous material. Width of specimen 3 mm. (Value range G)

Fig. 04-05. Murchison, fall September 1969, Murchison, Victoria, Australia. A CM2 carbonaceous chondrite, a type containing a maximum amount of organic material, approximately 2-4 percent. The black matrix contains a mix of organic compounds, including polycyclic aromatic hydrocarbons similar to those that compose coal tar (familiar if you have used a water based coal tar emulsion to coat a driveway). Other organic compounds include high molecular weight aliphatic hydrocarbons (asphalt-like material), amino acids, and alcohols. Amino acids had previously been detected in other carbonaceous meteorites such as Murray and Cold Bokkeveld, but it was suspected that they were a consequence of contamination from handling. The high organic content of Murchison gave clear evidence that amino acids found were indigenous to the meteorite and were not contamination. The greenish, circular structures scattered throughout are chondrules; other fragments are silicate clasts.

Fig. 04-06. Murchison. The fall of large stones of this meteorite in 1969 supplied sufficiently fresh and abundant material to quell any doubts that the organic compounds present were not indigenous to the meteorite. Small silicate chondrules scattered through the black, organic material containing matrix characterize these meteorites. Specimen 6 mm in length.

Fig. 04-09. Another specimen of Allende from the 1969 fall. Note the large number of chondrules in this fragment. 1969 was a capital year for astrogeology. The fall of the Allende meteorite put more fresh chondritic meteorites in the "hands" of scientists and collectors, and the Murchison meteorite also fell that year. These events were accompanied that same year by the first Apollo lunar exploration. (Value range F)

Fig. 04-07. Colony, Oklahoma, CO3.0 (find), 1975. A carbonaceous chondrite low in carbonaceous material such as in this meteorite can survive some weathering and be retrieved as a find rather than only as a fall. CM carbonaceous chondrites, with their friable or crumbly texture and organic components, weather very rapidly so they are never collected as a meteorite find. (Value range E)

Fig. 04-10. Saratov, Russia. Chondritic meteorite, fall 1918 (stony meteorite). This is a fresh specimen (a fall) of a L 4 chondritic meteorite, one of the most common of the stony meteorites. The chondrules in Saratov are small and relatively inconspicuous. Many L 4 chondrites are found in the Sahara Desert where they are collected by wandering locals. Like many stone meteorites collected as falls, this specimen is friable as can be seen from the small fragments which flaked off when the image of it was taken with a flat bed scanner. (Value range F)

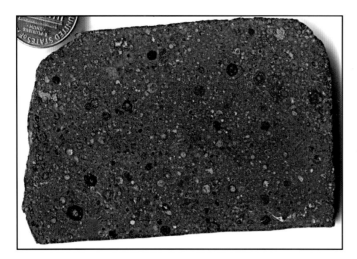

Fig. 04-08. Allende, CV3 carbonaceous chondrite. This is the most common carbonaceous meteorite available and normally seen. In 1969, a large group of stones fell near the Pueblito (village) de Allende in the state of Chihuahua, Mexico. The amount of carbonaceous material in this meteorite is lower than in other classes of carbonaceous meteorites, such as Murchison or Tagish Lake. CV3 meteorites like Allende are also less friable and crumbly than other carbonaceous meteorites. The spherical and subspherical components of this meteorite are chondrules; these can make up 75-80 percent of Allende. (Value range D)

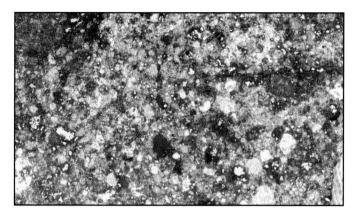

Fig. 04-11. NWA (Northwest Africa). A specimen of a typical L 4 chondritic meteorite found in the Sahara Desert of Northwest Africa. The extreme aridity of this region has preserved what are relatively fragile meteorites from weathering. Residence in the desert has resulted in their being much more durable than their counterparts collected as falls, which are usually crumbly and fragile. When analyzed, such stony meteorites contain very little organic material, however it can be detected in these samples as a product of terrestrial (earthly) contamination. Organic compounds in carbonaceous chondrites, first detected in 1835, were considered to be from terrestrial contamination until the 1969 fall of Murchison, a CV2 carbonaceous meteorite which proved without doubt that the organic components present in this meteorite were indeed indigenous to it. Northwest Africa (NWA) meteorites surfaced in great numbers in 2005 and have been distributed widely among meteorite collectors during the last few years. (Value range D,-F)

Fig. 04-13. Esquel, Argentina (pallasite). Green crystals are olivine or the gem stone peridot, which is set in a matrix of nickel iron. Meteorites like this contrast in their beauty with the black and drab carbonaceous meteorites. They represent high temperature conditions where the once molten olivine crystallized slowly after it separated from molten nickel-iron; like oil and water, the liquid olivine was immiscible with the molten metal. These and other metallic meteorites represent high temperature conditions that would negate any chance of survival of organic material, unlike the low temperature, accreted carbonaceous chrondrites. Such meteorites as this and related nickle-iron meteorites are younger than the chrondritic ones, which represent very primitive material from which the material of the solar system was derived. (Value range E)

Fig. 04-12. Siderite, Gibeon. A nickel-iron meteorite formed from the slow cooling of metal within an asteroids interior. The pattern of interlocked crystals is called Widmanstatten figures—an interlocking mass of large crystals of kamacite, an alloy made up of nickel and iron similar to stainless steel. This type of meteorite is made from material that was once in a molten state, a condition very different from that represented by the chondritic meteorites made up of compressed fragments, some of which came directly from the condensation of a nebula. (Value range E)

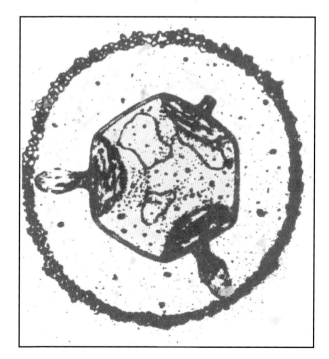

Fig. 04-14. Sketch of an organized element found under high magnification in a carbonaceous chondrite (Murray). Such very small objects are now believed to be small crystals, formed in a zero gravity field in a manner somewhat similar to that involved in the formation of snowflakes, which are small ice crystals. When originally found in the early 1950s, they were suggested to be microfossils representative of life that existed somewhere else in the Milky Way galaxy.

Fig. 04-15. A shadow image showing another version of an organized element, from the Orgueil meteorite, a carbonaceous chondrite that fell in France in the 1860s.

Fig. 04-17. The brown, rust-like material on this slice of a Northwest Africa (NWA) chondritic meteorite is a consequence of its earthly residence; it is rust formed from oxidization of metallic iron. Meteorites don't like the earth's atmosphere and its water. They react with it and change from their original cosmic composition. Considering that they have lain on the earth's surface for at least hundreds of years, NWA's meteorites are amazingly fresh. This could only happen in a very dry environment like that of the Sahara Desert or some other very dry terrestrial environment.

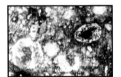

Fig. 04-18. Enlargement of two armored chondrules shown in the previous photo. Armored chondrules represent a "plating" of metal on the surface of the chondrule when it was suspended in space. The plating metal came from a nova of a dying star that predated the formation of the solar system.

Fig. 04-16. Portion of a typical NWA L-4 chondrite meteorite. A large clast (fragment) in the middle is rusted (iron has oxidized since entering the earth). Below this rusty clast are two small armored chondrules, peculiar chondrules that have been covered by a coating of nickel-iron. This might have been done just after the chondrule formed from condensation of vapors given off by a star in a nebula—the metallic armor on the chondrule forming by a blast of iron vapor from the same or possibly another star. The stars that existed in this nebula, some six billion years ago, no longer exist and this all happened before the solar system was formed.

Bibliography

Anders, Edward, and Frank W. Fitch. "Search for Organized Elements in Carbonaceous Chondrites." *Science* Vol. 182, 1966, pg. 781-790.

Bevan, Alex, and John de Laeter. *Meteorites: A Journey Through Space and Time*. Washington D.C. and London: Smithsonian Institution Press, 2002.

Norton, O. Richard. *Rocks From Space. Meteorites and Meteorite Hunters*. Missoula, Montana: Mountain Press Publishing Company, 1994.

Hutchison, Robert. *The Search for our Beginning*. British Museum (Natural History) and Oxford University Press, 1983.

Studier, Martin H., Ryoichi Hayatsu, and Edward Anders. "Organic Compounds in Carbonaceous Chondrites." *Science*, Vol. 149, 1965, p. 1455-58.

Urey, Harold C. "Biological Material in Meteorites: a Review." *Science*, Vol. 151, No. 3707, 1966, p. 157-166.

Chapter Five

The Archean and Stromatolites, The Most Ancient Fossils

Archean Sedimentary Rocks and Stromatolites

Archean rocks are usually hard; they generally make up very rocky terrain and don't look promising for yielding fossils. Fossils tracks, shells, and other invertebrate hard parts are totally absent. These, the most ancient rocks of the earth's crust, have been preserved over vast periods of time from erosion by having been pushed deep into the crust as a consequence of tectonic forces. Here they were "cooked" or metamorphosed to varying degrees, compressed, and shot through with various veins of quartz, aplite, and "spars."

Fig. 05-01. Archean metasediment intruded by granite dikes (white band) and quartz veins. Western Ontario. This is an Archean outcrop that shows the complexity and "confusion" represented by Archean terrains and the deep burial in the earth's crust to which they were subjected.

Fig. 05-02. Archean meta-siltstone and iron formation in Northwest Territories, Canada (Nonacho Lake), representing one of the oldest iron formations in North America. It consists of alternating layers of silty sediment, "dirty" sandstone, hematite, and jasper. The white "cracks" are quartz veins, commonly seen in many ancient terrestrial rocks that, in order to have been preserved for so long, had to be buried for a few billion years deep in the crust.

Fig. 05-03. Glacially scoured surface of Archean quartz pebble conglomerate, a distinctive and unique Archean rock type. Nonacho Lake, NWT Canada.

Fig. 05-04. Archean black slate outcrop on Trans Canada highway, western Ontario. As is usual for Archean strata, the bedding planes of this slaty shale are vertical.

Fig. 05-05. Dirty, carbon rich? sandstone beds (greywacke) in western Colorado near Steamboat Springs. Archean "sandstones" are usually dirty ones; clean sandstone is composed of sand that has been recycled many times through geologic processes. Archean sand, from the young earth, did not get the opportunity to be recycled many times and thus cleaned to become white sand.

Metamorphism and deep burial usually obliterates fossils or makes them subtle and difficult to distinguish from the enclosing rock. Stromatolites, however, can be tough, and while deep burial and metamorphism may blur them, their general form can still be retained. Even in consideration of their toughness, however, stromatolites are rare in Archean rocks. When present, Archean stromatolites are usually simple domes or broad, laminar forms. Archean stromatolites are rare, in part, because limestone and other carbonate rocks are rare in the Archean. The lack of Archean limestones seems to be primarily because during the early history of the earth, continents were small or did not exist and it is in shallow seas, covering parts of continents, that limestone and associated stromatolites form.

Tectonic activity (mountain building) in the Archean was on a scale vastly greater than it was during later geologic time. This was due to a greater supply of energy available, which in turn was due to greater amounts of radioactive elements decaying to give off thermal energy (the energy source of tectonic activity). Large land areas (continents) were either non-existent or small. Most of the earth consisted of "deep oceans" containing large amounts of dissolved iron salts, and in the early Archean (before life?), containing large amounts of "organic sludge," or what has been called a coacecervate. Those land areas that existed were small volcanic island arcs with little in the way of continental shelves. Continental shelves and shallow-water parts of the ocean underlain by continental crust are where limestone forms, and this is also where cyanobacteria thrive and happily build stromatolites; but these environments were mostly absent during the Archean. Moreover, some Archean stromatolites have a signature somewhat different from those of later geologic time and their biogenicity has been questioned.

Interpretations regarding those Archean stromatolites that do exist vary widely. Some have questioned their biogenic origin, in part, because it would extend the existence of life so deep into the earth's geologic past. Considering that the first billion years of earth history involved a molten and impacted surface, an environment inhospitable for prokaryotic life existing 3.5 billion years ago (the age of the oldest stromatolites) would leave little time for chemical evolution. Chemical evolution, like other forms of evolution, should require the passage of vast spans of time. A way around this is the suggestion that life came to earth from space, possibly carried as prokaryotic cells as part of an extra solar meteorite from another part of the galaxy. Proponents of such "panspermia" cite the early geochemical record of life in the form of graphite beds and BIF, and that even though the occurrence of life is extraordinary, with the passage of vast spans of time an extraordinary or improbable event, like the appearance of life, can become probable.

Stromatolites occur in rocks 3.5 billion years old and banded iron formation (BIF), also suggestive of primitive photosynthetic life, occurs in even older rocks. There are only around fifteen known Archean stromatolite occurrences in the world, and these consist primarily of simple domes, laminar forms, or simple "fingers." Large and complex stromatolites, such as those found in the Proterozoic, are absent in the Archean. Microbes responsible for Archean stromatolites generally are considered to have been cocoid cyanobacteria, some forms of filamentous cyanobacteria, and photosynthetic bacteria.

Fig. 05-06. Metamorphosed iron formation near Flin Flon, Manitoba. As is usual with Archean rocks, bedding planes (layers) are on end or are vertical. This strata is similar to metamorphosed iron formation of the Isua Series (Supracrustals) of southwestern Greenland, the oldest known rock sequence on earth. These beds of metamorphosed iron formation, like that from the nearly 4 billion year old Isua series of Greenland, may have formed from non-photosynthetically produced oxygen formed by photo-dissociation. Most Archean BIF, however, is considered to have been a product formed from the oxygen given off by photosynthesis. Such oxygen, besides being lethal to many microbial life forms like the anaerobic bacteria, would have reacted with soluble ferrous iron dissolved in sea water, precipitating it as insoluble ferric oxide to form thick beds of iron formation.

Fig. 05-07. Outcrops of the Archean Soudan iron formation near the town of Ely in northern Minnesota. The Archean strata shown here is a typical BIF, or banded iron formation. The white bands are white chert, the grey bands are hematite, and the reddish jasper. Archean terrains themselves invoke feelings of ancient, somewhat mysterious and brooding moods connected to their complex and long geologic history.

Fig. 05-08. Early Precambrian (Archean) rocks often contain sizeable amounts of disseminated carbon or graphite; the question arises as to what was the source of the carbon in these early rocks. One explanation is that it is of biogenic origin, perhaps originating as carbon that constituted the biomass of vast numbers of bacteria. An alternative explanation is that the graphite came from non-biogenic sources; possibly a mix of organic components produced by a process such as that involved with the Miller Experiment. Such a mix of inorganically produced compounds made from chemical reactions in an oxygen free environment is called a **coacecervate**. Some geoscientists have suggested that Archean oceans, particular those of the early Archean, became a sort of organic-rich "soup" of amino acids produced through non-biogenic means. Incorporated into sea floor sediments, this carbonaceous matter became the source of the disseminated graphite. Outcrop on Trans-Canada Highway, western Ontario.

Fig. 05-09. Black, iron and carbon? rich metamorphosed dirty sandstone (greywacke), intruded by granite (white), typical Archean outcrop with vertical beds. Trans-Canada Highway, western Ontario.

Archean sedimentary rocks are different from those of later geologic time! Sedimentary rocks represent sediments that are a product of conditions existing at the earth's surface when the sediments were deposited; they form by interaction with a planet's atmosphere. The fact that Archean rocks are different from younger sedimentary rocks suggests that fundamental surface conditions of the early earth were different from those of today.

Most shales (now slates) of the Archean are carbon-rich, containing carbon in the form of graphite. It has been stated that 70+ percent of the earth's carbon has been locked up (sequestered) in Archean sedimentary rocks. This represents a huge amount of carbon that was probably removed from an early carbon dioxide atmosphere by early photosynthetic life. The Archean earth probably had an atmosphere composed of carbon dioxide and water vapor. The earth's first atmosphere, one that was presumably lost prior to the Archean, is believed to have been rich in hydrogen and helium, elements that today are essentially non-existent in the atmosphere. Hydrogen is rare in its elemental state, helium is non-existent on the earth. The second atmosphere, that of the Archean, contained little or no oxygen and was made up primarily of carbon dioxide, nitrogen, and water vapor. Such an atmosphere would have resulted in high atmospheric temperatures because of the greenhouse effect. There is astrophysical evidence suggesting that such higher temperatures on the earth would have been counteracted by the sun being less intense four+ billion years ago. The planet Venus, with its carbon dioxide rich atmosphere and runaway greenhouse effect (although without earth's oceans), is a reasonable comparison to the early earth. The earth acquired life, Venus didn't.

Fig. 05-10. Black, carbon-rich slate of Archean age in the Black Hills, South Dakota. High carbon content in the form of graphite is characteristic of many Archean sedimentary rocks. The carbon in this rock probably came from a biogenic source, however some have suggested that it might have been formed from inorganically produced "organic" compounds, like those of the Miller Experiment, which formed a type of organic soup (coacecervate) of the oceans of the early earth. These rocks have been intruded with granites that date to some 2.1 billion years old and is the granite that composes Mt. Rushmore.

Fig. 05-11. Archean black chert and/or greywacke, intruded by pink granite. Flin Flon, Manitoba, Canada.

Fig. 05-13. Graphite, originally of organic origin, can also occur as distinct crystals in Archean and other highly metamorphosed rocks. The back mineral in this coarsely crystalline marble is graphite, probably originally from cyanobacteria or other monerans. (Value range H)

A unique Archean sedimentary rock consists of thick sequences of quartz pebble conglomerate. These conglomerates are found as massive accumulations (sometimes miles in thickness) of rounded gravel made up of quartz and granite pebbles, and are unlike conglomerate deposits found in later geologic time. Such "quartz pebble conglomerates" represent something unique about the Archean earth, as quartz pebble conglomerate like that found in the Archean is absent in younger strata.

Fig. 05-12. Archean graphite bearing schist. Highly metamorphosed, this graphite bearing schist was once a black, carbonaceous (carbon bearing) shale. Intense pressure (a consequence of deep burial within the earth's crust) accompanied by tectonic forces caused the black shale to crystallize and become schist. Blacks specks are graphite, white is quartz and feldspar crystals. Ashland graphite schist, Appalachians of Alabama.

Fig. 05-14. Quartz pebble (with granite and gneiss pebbles) conglomerate. Such rock made up of pebbles can form very thick sequences of strata in the Archean. Nothing like this, with such great thickness of conglomerate beds, occurs in younger geologic strata and/or terrains. This rock is quarried in Brazil and used worldwide for decorative stone. (Value range H)

Fig. 05-15. Two tiles of Archean pebble conglomerate from Brazil. Polished Archean pebble conglomerate like this is sold as a type of "granite" and used in countertops, floors, and other commercial and domestic uses. The tile to the right contains a quartzite cobble containing white quartz veins. Many Archean rocks like this are different from those of later geologic time. James Hutton's 1795 statement regarding the geologic record, "I see no vestige of a beginning and no prospect of an end," is not totally correct with respect to the Archean. Archean rocks are different because they were formed nearer the beginning of the earth at a time when conditions **were** vastly different from those of later geologic time. There is a vestige of a beginning with some Archean rocks! (Value range G)

Some geologists consider the much greater amount of tectonic activity in the Archean, powered by heat energy given off by radioactive decay, to be the reason for these thick sequences of quartz pebble conglomerate. In the Archean earth, greater amounts of radioactive isotopes such as Uranium 235, Potassium 40, and other radioactive elements existed. Decay of these radioactive elements in the earth produced internal heat of a magnitude much greater than that of today's earth. Tectonic activity is driven by this internal heat, so with higher levels of radioactivity, mountain building would be expected to reach quite higher levels than it does today.

The Archean earth had no continents, only small island arcs representing the bare beginnings of continents. Due to the greater amounts of tectonic activity powered by greater amounts of radioactivity, these island arcs included mountains that extended into the stratosphere—mountains possibly some twenty-five to thirty miles high above the ocean's floor. The products of weathering associated with such mountains should be different in size from that produced by the more modest mountains of today and more recent geologic time. Weathering today produces large quantities of sand, some of which is cemented together to form beds of sandstone. Weathering in thirty-mile high mountains, however, would produce gravel in great quantities as the principal weathering product, rather than sand. Sand, usually of a dirty type, is found as minor layers, which are dwarfed by the thick beds of coarser particles forming the quartz pebble conglomerates.

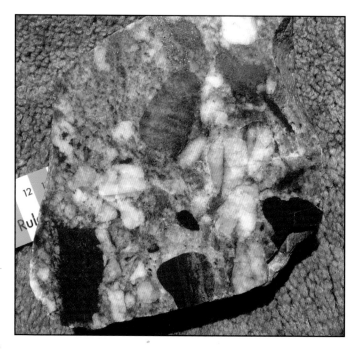

Fig. 05-16. Archean (or possibly early Paleoproterozoic) slab of quartz pebble conglomerate. Quartz pebbles comprise the majority of the clasts of this rock, along with pebbles of iron formation. Great thicknesses of this rock occur in the Archean, such as at Los Pinos Canyon of the Los Pinos River near Vallecito Reservoir, southwest Colorado, where this specimen came from. (Value range G)

The oldest known fossils are stromatolites that come from a sequence of rock strata that is 3.5 billion years old and found at a remote place nicknamed "North Pole" in northwestern Western Australia. These occur in the Warrawoona Group, a sequence of iron formation, chert, and lavas that comprise a very ancient part of Australia called the Pilbara Block. Except for their great antiquity, 3.5 billion years and partial preservation in barite, these stromatolites look very much like the stromatolites found in younger rocks.

The oldest known earth rocks are metamorphosed strata of the Isua Series of Greenland. Isua series rocks include highly metamorphosed banded iron formation as well as other highly metamorphosed sediments. Banded iron formation this far back into "deep time," like other BIFs, probably indicates the existence of photosynthetic life, possibly photosynthetic bacteria. It is also possible, however, that oxygen involved in the formation of these unique rocks may have come from photo-dissociation of water, rather than from photosynthesis. Such free oxygen is a non-biogenic source of oxygen. Oxygen produced by photo-dissociation is probably the source of the oxygen that combined with iron on the surface of Mars to produce the red oxide (hematite) characteristic of that planet.

Another sedimentary rock associated with the early earth is greywacke, a dirty, iron-rich type of sandy sediment. Over long spans of geologic time such dirty, sandy material is recycled and cleaned to form the beds of quartz sandstone and the quartz beach and river sands so commonly seen on the continents today.

Archean sandstone, by contrast, is "dirty," containing a lot of silt, igneous particles, and clay, which, on the early earth, had not yet had time to be cleaned. This dirty sandstone is usually interbedded with quartz pebble conglomerate and again has a signature different from younger rocks of a similar type.

Iron Formation or Banded Iron Formation (BIF)

The sedimentary rock called iron formation or banded iron formation (BIF) is another distinctive Archean rock. BIF usually consists of a mixture of sedimentary quartz (chert), beds of hematite or other iron compounds, and jasper (an intimate mixture of hematite and quartz).

This sedimentary rock type, common in the Archean, consists of alternating thin layers of hematite (or magnetite), jasper, and quartz. It's a rock type seldom found in strata younger than 1.5 billion years old and therefore is nearly unique to the Archean and the early Proterozoic—that is, the early earth. Banded iron formation (BIF) is the source of much of the world's iron ore. The iron ore occurrences of the Lake Superior region of the United States and Canada, Labrador, Brazil, South Africa, and Australia are derived from BIF.

Archean BIF is often finely banded, with the bands often contorted. Proterozoic iron formation usually is not so banded and sometimes exhibits well-formed stromatolites (see Chapter Six). Obvious stromatolites, by contrast, are usually lacking in Archean BIF, possibly because it was deposited in deep waters where the photosynthetic monerans responsible for BIF were suspended in the water column near the ocean's surface and not able to live on a substrate, as did moneran communities of the shallower waters of the Proterozoic.

Fig. 05-17. Granite gneiss pebbles in arkosic matrix—a decorative tile cut from these distinctive and peculiar rocks of the Archean. The fact that such conglomerates occur in very thick sequences that do not occur in this manner in younger sequences suggest that unique conditions existed in the early earth. It has been suggested that such pebbles are the product of weathering of extremely high mountains which existed on the early earth. Very thick beds of pebbles (the equivalent of sand coming from the weathering of modern mountains) accumulated at the foot of these Archean mountains to form this conglomerate. (Value range G)

Fig. 05-18. Domal stromatolite from the 3.5 billion year old Warrawoona Group near North Pole, Australia. This is one of the oldest known stromatolites. Specimen on display at U.S. National Museum, Smithsonian Institution, Washington D. C.

Fig. 05-19. Boulder of banded iron formation, specifically the Soudan iron formation laid into a wall. Such Archean iron formation is or has been mined for hematite in northern Minnesota and other places where Archean iron formation occurs. Unlike younger Proterozoic iron formations like the Gunflint or Biwabik, the Soudan iron formation has not yielded distinct stromatolites, but is probably biogenic in origin. Iron formation is another rock type more or less restricted to the geologic record of the early earth.

Fig. 05-20. Glacial boulder of banded iron formation (BIF), northern Quebec. Probably from the Sokoman Iron Formation of the Labrador Trough. Such boulders of iron formation can be carried long distances by the continental glaciers of the geologically recent (Pleistocene) ice age.

Fig. 05-21. 3.5 ga (billion years) old cobble of banded iron formation from Australia. The black bands are hematite, red bands are jasper, white is quartz, and the yellow is "tiger's eye." These various colored bands were originally produced as a consequence of precipitation of iron oxide from photosynthetic bacteria and cyanobacteria. Such microbes lived in the water column of a 3+ billion year old ocean at a time when the earth's atmosphere contained little or no free oxygen. Such colorful types of iron formation are sometimes used as semi-precious gemstone materials and are known as "tiger iron." (Value range G)

The origin of iron formation, like so much ancient geologic phenomena, is hotly debated. BIF is generally attributed to being a product of the chemistry that accompanied the transition of the earth's atmosphere from a reducing or anoxic (oxygen free) one to one containing elemental oxygen. The geochemistry that produced iron formation is fairly simple; it involves the fact that in an anoxic atmosphere, ferrous iron would accumulate in the oceans from the weathering of rocks. Such ferrous iron is highly soluble in seawater and would accumulate with time if not removed (as is the case with sodium and potassium in the oceans of today). Free or elemental oxygen, produced in small quantities by photo-dissociation, would, when dissolved in seawater, combine with the dissolved ferrous iron and then precipitate on the ocean floor as an iron rich sediment. The thin bands of iron formation of the early Archean, as well as the hematite on Mars, may have had their origin in this manner.

When photosynthesis came upon the scene, which it did on the early earth after a period of intense meteorite and asteroid bombardment ended, amounts of available elemental oxygen increased greatly. This in turn caused the precipitation of larger amounts of ferric iron, which had been accumulating in the waters of the oceans as the soluble ferrous iron. Such biogenically precipitated ferric oxide now forms the thick beds of iron oxide or BIF of the middle and late Archean.

Deposition of iron formation continued into the middle part of the Proterozoic Era (Mesoproterozoic) and ceased only when all of the ferrous iron in the world's oceans was removed, at which time elemental oxygen began to accumulate in the atmosphere; this was about 1.4 billion years ago.

Fig. 05-23. Iron formation or jasper "eggs" from western Australia. Such eggs, frequently seen in rock shops and tourist outlets, can be both inexpensive and scientifically interesting. (Value range G)

Fig. 05-24. BIF eggs (banded iron formation). Such egg shaped, polished pieces of BIF are sometimes found in rock and novelty shops as well as on eBay. The BIF is usually from Archean beds of western Australia, an area of very ancient rocks. (Value range G)

Fig. 05-22. Another boulder of 3-2-3.5 billion year old iron formation cemented into a wall. Iron formation boulders, found in glacial deposits of the Midwestern United States, are sometimes singled out for masonry work as they are attractive and different looking from most other rocks. Fingers are pointing to grey hematite, which can in some iron formation deposits be concentrated enough to form industrial iron ore. The boulder shown here has the distinctive signature of the Archean Soudan Iron Formation and was carried southward by continental glaciers some two million years ago.

Fig. 05-27. Slab of banded iron formation (BIF) from the Archean of western Australia. The yellow band is a layer of quartz which replaced amphibole crystals, a phenomena sometimes associated with Archean beds of banded iron formation. Such "tiger iron" is made into semiprecious jewelry such as necklaces and earrings. (Value range G)

Fig. 05-25 and 05-26. BIF spheres. Polished spheres of banded iron formation from Australia are attractive. The red layers are jasper, the black is hematite, and the yellow quartz, which has replaced crysotile (tiger's eye). These spheres are frequently seen in rock shops and are generally more expensive than the eggs. (Value range G or F depending upon size of sphere).

Fig. 05-28. Slab of banded iron formation in which the jasper, rather than being red, is yellow. From Archean rocks outcropping near Espanola, central Ontario, Canada.

Fig. 05-29. Boulder of BIF cemented into a wall. Layering or bedding in Archean BIF is often somewhat irregular like this.

Peculiarities of Archean Stromatolites

Unlike Proterozoic and Phanerozoic stromatolites, the very ancient ones of the Archean are rare and somewhat plain. What is often seen in the Archean are laminar stromatolites, which have a rock signature referred to as crypt-algal laminae. Sometimes, such laminae form the dome or "fingers" of a typical stromatolite, but in most Archean occurrences, one is more likely to encounter just laminar forms. With such laminar stromatolites, defining what distinguishes the signature of algal or microbial growth from that produced by non-biogenic sediments can be tricky. If microfossils of the original single celled organism or algal filaments can be found under high magnification, then the structure is biogenic, however deep burial in the earth's crust and accompanying metamorphism usually destroys such microfossils and may blur the crypt-algal signature as well. Microbial laminates can be fine grained and usually possess slight crenulations. The laminae can be draped, folded, or abruptly broken when part of a microbial mat is fractured. Laminae above and below a layer are connected to each other by supports, and between the supports are voids that usually are filled with crystalline material such as calcite or quartz. This framework of supports, laminae, and voids is what gives the characteristic "signature" to a microbial mat and to stromatolites, and is referred to as a stromatolitic fabric.

Fig. 05-30. Wawa, Ontario stromatolite-1. Some Archean stromatolites like these are problematic and peculiar. These structures, were found in an iron carbonate (siderite) layer in an underground iron mine near Wawa, Ontario, at the eastern end of Lake Superior. They are puzzling in many ways, as are many Archean stromatolites, but are probably bonafide stromatolites. They resemble concretions in other ways and don't have a microbial signature. This is a consequence of the rocks' metamorphism during deep burial in the earth's crust, a necessary condition to preserve such ancient rock layers through long periods of geologic time. The yellow crystals scattered throughout the structure are pyrite. (Value range E)

Fig. 05-31. Wawa stromatolite-2. These are found in an iron carbonate layer at the 1,000 ft. level of the now closed iron mine at Wawa, Ontario, at the eastern end of Lake Superior. (Value range F)

Fig. 05-32. A broad domal stromatolite from the late Archean Steep Rock Lake Limestone, Atikokan, Ontario. Stromatolites from ancient stromatolite-rich limestones crop out north of the town of Atikokan and have a crypt algal, stromatolitic fabric. White cracks at right are quartz veins. (Value range G)

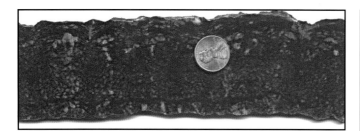

Fig. 05-33. Small domal stromatolites run across the top of this black limestone bed of the Archean Steep Rock Lake Limestone near Atikokan, Ontario. These stromatolites and the limestone with which they are associated have a distinctive pampilist or "chicken wire" fabric, which is also seen in similar Archean stromatolites from Zaire, central Africa.

Fig. 05-34. *Atikokania* sp. A large slab with the radiating "needles" of the pseudofossil or dubiofossil *Atikokania*. Part of the stromatolite shown in the previous photo can be seen at the right portion of the slab. Specimen from the now reclaimed Steep rock Lake Iron Mine. Steep Rock Lake Limestone, Atikokan, Ontario.

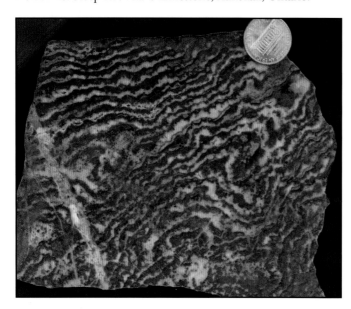

Fig. 05-35. Laminar stromatolite made up of small stromatolite domes. This is part of some very large stromatolites (shown in the next photo), formerly exposed in the Steep Rock Lake Iron Mine. Atikokan, Ontario. (Value range G)

Fig. 05-36. Giant domal stromatolites formerly exposed in the now reclaimed and water filled Steep Rock Lake Iron Mine. Atikokan, Ontario.

Fig. 05-37. Slice through portion of one of the gigantic stromatolites shown in previous photo. This cross section shows stromatolitic laminae which themselves form domes as well as very small domes that converge into the crypt-algal structure. Steep Rock Lake Iron Mine, Atikokan, Ontario, Canada.

Some Archean stromatolites lack a microbial mat signature. Whether this is a consequence of their not being of biogenic origin is debated; metamorphism usually destroys this signature. It's a significant debate, however, as Archean stromatolite occurrences form the benchmarks for the earliest occurrences of life.

This biogenic versus non-biogenic argument is the same one first introduced in the nineteenth century with Eozoon, and also surfaced in the 1950s with the organized elements of the carbonaceous meteorites.

Archean stromatolites and cryptalgal laminates have been painstakingly examined for the presence of the microbes that presumably produced them. With considerable searching under high magnification, oil immersion microscopy, convincing filaments and coccoid spheres have been found, but they are rare. Known Archean microfossils are paltry in comparison to the richness and diversity of those found with younger stromatolites. Such a scarcity of microfossils can be explained for the same reason that explains the general absence of Archean stromatolitic fabric—it has been destroyed by metamorphism accompanying deep burial in the earth's crust. Unlike stromatolites themselves, which are tough, the fabric of a stromatolite and any accompanying microfossils are delicate, so that crystallization during metamorphism usually obliterates them.

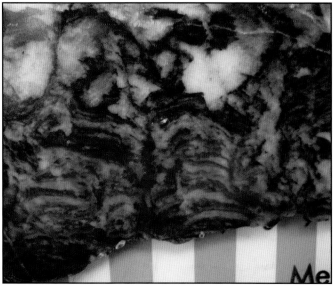

Fig. 05-38. Stromatolitic laminae in black; white areas are calcite and quartz filled voids in a portion of a large Archean stromatolite reef. The white areas in the original reef may have been filled with mucilage, a material commonly secreted by cyanobacteria that makes rocks coated with modern algae so slippery. (Value range G)

Fig. 05-39. Black limestone, bearing a diverse variety of stromatolites cropout in far western Ontario, where they are associated with iron formation that was formerly mined. This specimen of the stromatolite form genus *Kussiella* is characteristic of the Archean and the Paleoproterozoic, that is, that part of earth history some 2.5 billion years ago. A slightly laminated structure on this slab occurs in the upper left. This non-stromatolitic signature may be part of either a hot spring or an evaporate deposit. *Atikokania*, with which this stromatolite is associated, is considered to be formed by crystals formed under desiccating conditions in the shallow waters of a tidal pool.

Fig. 05-40. This assemblage of stromatolites includes the black, non-laminated dome which is probably a bacterial stromatolite. Photosynthetic bacteria can produce such compact (and usually dark colored) stromatolites. Mottled (pampilist) patterns above the bacterial strom probably represent a scattering of cyanobacteria clumps and cavities, the latter possibly originally being filled with gypsum crystals. This represents a texture that is characteristic of many Archean stromatolites. Steep Rock Lake Limestone, Atikokan, Ontario. (Note paper clip at left for scale.) (Value range F).

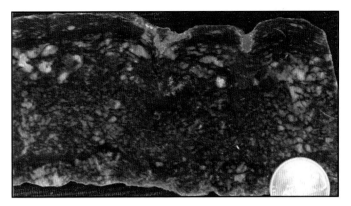

Fig. 05-41. Another slab of Steep Rock Lake stromatolites with pampilist structure. (Value range F)

Fig. 05-42. Slice through a domal stromatolite with coarse laminate structure. This stromatolite is high in iron and formed in a highly anaerobic (reducing) environment, a characteristic of many Archean stromatolites. Proterozoic stromatolites are usually more oxidized, with the reddish or pinkish colors of oxidized iron oxide (hematite). The honey colored inclusion is crystalline dolomite, which fills cavities possibly produced by gas eruptions in the highly anaerobic environment in which the stromatolite grew. Similar cavities and fillings are found in other Archean stromatolites. This specimen as well as the rest of the Archean stromatolites were found in a glacial erratic in northeast Missouri. They were probably transported southward from Archean greenstone belts of the Lake Superior region of northern Minnesota or western Ontario. (Value range F)

Fig. 05-43. *Kussiella* sp. A large digitate stromatolite from part of a large glacial erratic apparently from Archean greenstone belts of northern Minnesota or western Ontario, possibly excavated and carried southward by Pleistocene glaciers from the area now occupied by Lake Superior. These stromatolites appear similar to those from the 2.65 billion year old Steep Rock Lake Limestone of western Ontario and may be from the same greenstone belt. A series of mid to late Archean greenstone belts extend across northern Minnesota and western Ontario. These are most likely the source of greenstone and banded iron formation boulders (Fig. 05-22) also found in glacial drift south of these greenstone belts, which occur in the ancient Superior Province of the Canadian Shield. (Value range E)

Fig. 05-44. Another section through the same stromatolite as in previous photo. These stromatolites grew on a substrate of layered bluish siltstone. Note the similarity of these stromatolites to those shown in Fig. 05-40. They are also quite similar to mid-Archean stromatolites of the Bulawayan Group, Bulawayan Greenstone Belt, Zimbabwe, which until stromatolites were found in the early Archean Warrawoona Group of the Pilbara Block of Western Australia (Fig. 05-18), were the oldest known fossils. Archean stromatolites are usually black or grey in contrast to Proterozoic and Phanerozoic ones, which are often more colorful. (Value range E)

Fig. 05-45. Laminar stromatolite from the same stromatolite reef as in the previous two photos. "Chicken wire" structure in middle of view is characteristic of many Archean stromatolites, including those from the 2.65 billion year old Steep Rock Limestone, which this and above stromatolites may correlate with. The digitate stromatolites shown in Fig. 05-43 grew on this as a substrate.

Fig. 05-47. Weathered surface of a large domal stromatolite from part of a stromatolite reef probably carried southward by glaciers from the region of Lake Superior. Figs. 05-42 and 05-46 are cut and polished sections of this stromatolite. (Value range E)

Fig. 05-46. Large slice through part of the stromatolite reef of the previous photos. This slice shows the top of digitate forms (Kussiella), upon which grew larger domal stromatolites. These domes are the same as those shown in Fig. 05-42 and are similar to stromatolites from the Steep Rock Lake Limestone as well as Archean stromatolites from the Bulawayan Greenstone Belt, Zimbabwe. (Value range E)

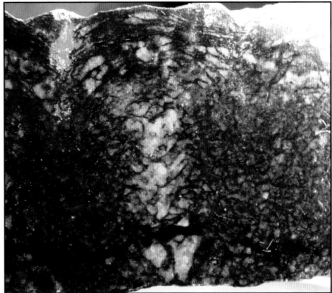

Fig. 05-48. Slice through small domes of a Steep Rock stromatolite with distinctive "chicken wire" or pampilist structure. This is believed to have formed from stromatolite growth under warm or even hot conditions in shallow water. Such "chicken wire" structure is believed to be associated with gypsum crystals, a mineral that forms under conditions of high rates of evaporation of sea water. Streep Rock Lake Limestone, Atikokan Ontario. Archean stromatolites are believed to have formed primarly around the margins of volcanic islands that later became the nucleus of protocontinents. (Value range G)

Fig. 05-49. An "egg" and a heart made from a distinctive type of Archean laminar stromatolite found in western Australia. (Value range G, each specimen)

Fig. 05-50. Laminar stromatolite. This "signature" of a laminar stromatolite is distinctive and characteristic of the mid-Archean. The red laminar stroms in the previous photo have this same signature and are of similar age, yet these two specimens come from half a world apart. In the Archean Era, the places where these stromatolites grew may have been in the same area, perhaps from the same island arc. mid-Archean, Schreiber, Ontario.

Fig. 05-51. *Conophyton* sp. A type of stromatolite consisting of nested cones can be indicative of moneran communities growing in association with geothermal water (hot springs). The form genus *Conophyton* is found in the Archean as well as in younger rock strata. Its presence in the Archean suggests an amount of geothermal energy that was more extensive in the early earth. With the early earth, there were greater amounts of radioactive isotopes giving off heat than later in the earth's history or today. (Value range G)

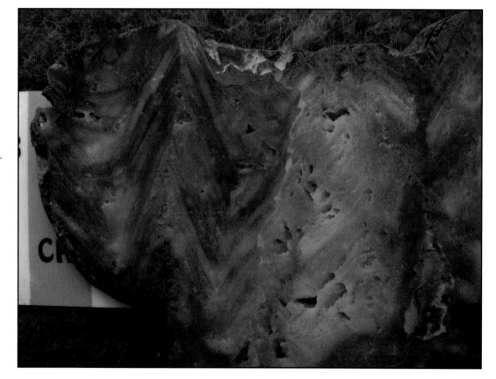

Atikokania

A peculiar fossil-like structure (dubiofossil) found in Archean rocks of the Canadian Shield is named after the western Ontario town of Atikokan. Originally described by Charles Walcott, *Atikokania* was considered as a type of archeocyathid. Archeocyathids are themselves puzzling fossils, having no direct re-lationship with living organisms and restricted to the earliest part of the Cambrian Period. *Atikokania* occurs associated with well-formed stromatolites, sometimes consisting of sprays of radiating needles clustered between stromatolite "fingers." Like *Eozoon canadense*, the affinity of *Atikokania* has been argued in the scientific literature, however majority opinion holds today that it is a pseudofossil—a form of radiating crystals, probably originally aragonite or gypsum, growing in a hypersaline environment associated with Archean volcanic island arcs. Similar structures are seen in much younger limestones formed under similar hypersaline conditions.

The pseudofossil Eozoon, when observed in outcrop on a rocky hillside, forms reef-like masses lying upon masses of diopside, a high temperature silicate mineral. It took a lot of argument and "arm waving" for science to agree on Eozoon's pseudofossil designation. It is often difficult to distinguish a group of crystals that have grown together in clusters from forms taken by a group of primitive animals such as sponges, corals, fungi, or other radially symmetrical organisms that also grow in clusters. This is particularly true if the rocks containing such structures have been changed (metamorphosed) by pressure, as is the case with most Archean sedimentary rocks. Problematic, fossil-like structures are associated with stromatolites, which, until the 1960s, were themselves doubted by some paleontologists as being of biogenic origin. Sometimes the pseudofossils found in ancient Archean rocks look more organic than do associated stromatolites. Finding these objects to be biogenic has profound consequences as to the antiquity of life, its origin, and its distribution throughout the galaxy.

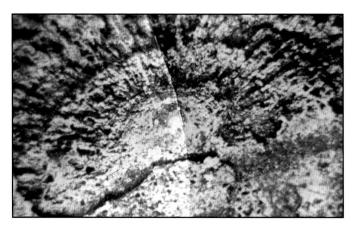

Fig. 05-52. Original illustration of Atikokania from C. D. Walcott's 1912 paper on the Steep Rock Lake fossils and Atikokania.

Fig. 05-54. Polished "cobble" of Atikokania from glacial drift, northern Minnesota. Criticism has been directed toward inclusion in a work of this type what is a unique(?) occurrence of this problematic structure. Atikokania occurs at localities other than the Steep Rock Lake occurrence and, like this specimen, has been found in glacial drift. The glaciers of the geologic recent ice age (Pleistocene Epoch) distributed rock over a sizeable portion of North America from a large portion of the Canadian Shield. Sometimes, specimens such as this occur in glacial drift, having been carried hundreds of miles from their original source. (Value range G)

Fig. 05-53. Polished slab of Atikokania. Notice pampilist structure surrounding it, a characteristic of many Archean stromatolites. (Value range G)

Fig. 05-55. Another slice through a spray of Atikokania. Steep Rock Limestone, Atikokan Ontario. (Value range G)

Fig. 05-56. *Atikokania* is a pseudofossil or a dubiofossil, probably formed from quartz replaced sprays of gypsum crystals. These occur as clusters in 2.8 billion year old limestone that crops out near the western Ontario town of Atikokan. *Atikokania* was originally considered by C. D. Walcott to be a type of very early sponge or an archeocyathid. (Value range G)

Fig. 05-58. "Widespread they stand, the northlands dusky forests, ancient, foreboding, etc." This literary quote from the manuscript of "Tapiola," a musical tone poem of the north by J. Sibelius, expresses a mood evoked by some of the earth's oldest rocks—such as are present in this view on the Canadian Shield. Archean rocks will be found along the edges of such lakes where bedding of strata will be vertical. Archean rocks and associated terrains reflect a subtle majesty, which echoes in turn, an immensity of time even for geology. Subtle moods induced by and associated with these ancient rocks and terrains can be sampled through the music Sibelius; try the 1st or 4th symphonies, "Tapiola," or "The Swan of Tuonela" from Lemminkainen Legends.

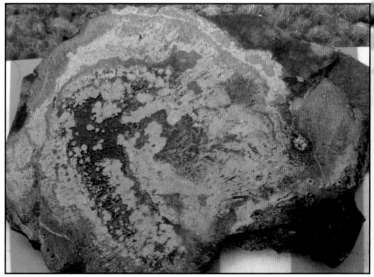

Fig. 05-57. Another rounded "mass" of Atikokania. This pseudofossil occurs in Archean Limestones of the Atikokan, Ontario-International Falls, Minnesota area of the Canadian Shield. It occurs between stromatolite domes and has confused many paleontologists for decades, including Charles D. Walcott. Similar structures are found in younger geologic strata that are the product of the growth of crystals, usually crystals of gypsum which grew under periodically dry conditions. *Atikokania* is considered to have had the same gypsum-crystal origin. Glacial erratic, northern Minnesota. (Value range G)

Fig. 05-59. A slice through another small Atikokania specimen, associated with stromatolites from the Steep Rock Lake Limestones. (Value range G)

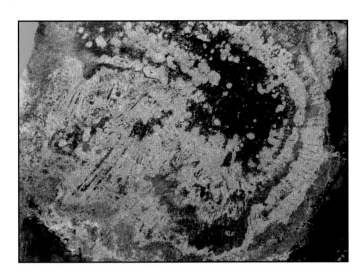

Fig. 05-60. Another sliced Atikokania specimen.

Fig. 05-61. Archean outcrop in Wyoming, probably the same age as the Steep Rock Lake Limestones or the Archean microfossils shown in Fig. 05-67, which came from nearby outcrops.

Fig. 05-63. A peculiar iron formation occurrence, which bears patterns suggestive of aberrant stromatolites. The outcrop from which this comes is an isolated one in central Wisconsin. It has the "signature" of an Archean iron formation and has circulated through the fossil market. (Value range G)

Fig. 05-64. Cabochon of BIF with some tiger's eye (known in the lapidary field as tiger iron). The fine bands are similar to the fine bands seen in Fig. 05-62. They may be of biogenic origin. Similar fine lamina (cryptalgal laminae) have yielded small carbon spheres, the presumed microfossils of moneran cells. The fine laminae are from an iron rich precipitate coming from either photosynthetic bacteria or from cyanobacteria. Western Australia. (Value range G)

Fig. 05-62. Possible moneran mats (yellow) associated with fine volcanic ash and found associated with an Archean volcanic tuff, Northern Minnesota. Similar, very fine lamina in black cherts associated with these tuffs have yielded small blobs of carbon, suggestive of groups of degraded moneran cells.

Fig. 05-65. Cabochon of BIF with yellow jasper (ocher pigmented) and speckled layers of Archean iron formation, western Australia. A variety of these interesting iron formation (tiger iron) cabochons are available on the rockhound market. (Value range G)

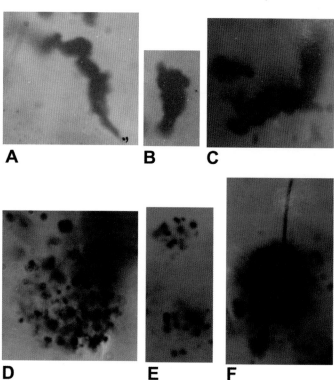

Fig. 05-67. Microfossils from Archean black cherts, These may be concentrations of degraded moneran cells or they may represent organic material (now carbon) from an organic rich "soup" of the early earth. Black, sometimes stromatolitic cherts of Archean age will show such microstructures; interpreting them is another matter! A-C, Elongate "puffy" carbonaceous inclusions; D-F, Cellular(?) clusters; F has a narrow filament(?) associated with it. Ferris Mts., Wyoming.

Fig. 05-66. Cabochon made from oxidized BIF with fine laminae (cryptalgal laminae) making "swirls" that suggest stromatolites. Fine laminae like this, in black, unoxidized iron formation under high magnification, can show small spheres and black specks. These are interpreted to be the carbonized remains of single celled monerans or may be from organic rich "soup" of the early earth. Oxidized BIF, like in this cabochon, normally do not exhibit this, presumably because an oxidizing environment destroyed them. (Value range G)

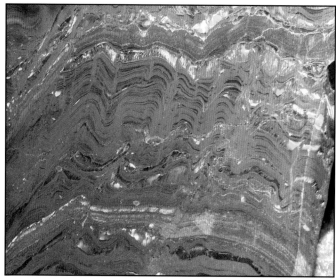

Fig. 05-68. Polished surface with fine micro lamina, probably of biogenic (moneran) origin suggestive of stromatolites. The red is jasper and the yellow is tiger's eye, which is exclusively associated with Archean iron formation. This slab is from western Australia where similar material is referred to in the rockhound market as tiger iron. (Value range F)

Bibliography

Barghoorn, Elso S., and J. William Schopf. "Microorganisms three billion years old from the Precambrian of South Africa." *Science*, Vol. 152, 1966.

Knoll, Andrew H. *Life on a Young Planet: The First Three Billion Years of Evolution on Earth*. Princeton, New Jersey: Princeton University Press, 2003.

Monastersky, Richard. "The Rise of Life on Earth." *National Geographic*, March 1998. pp 54-81.

Nisbet, E. G.. *The Young Earth: An Introduction to Archean Geology*. Boston: Allen and Unwin, 1987.

Schopf, J. William (ed.). *Earth's Earliest Biosphere: Its Origin and Evolution*. Princeton, New Jersey: Princeton University Press, 1983.

Schopf, J. William. "Microfossils of the Early Archean Apex Chert: New Evidence of the Antiquity of Life." *Science*, Vol. 260, 1993, pp. 640-646.

Walter, Malcolm R. "Archean Stromatolites: Evidence of the Earth's Earliest Benthos," in Schopf, J. William (ed.), *Earth's Earliest Biosphere: Its Origin and Evolution*. Princeton, New Jersey: Princeton University Press, 1983.

Chapter Six

The Paleoproterozoic—More Stromatolites!

Considerable confusion, to say the least, accompanies the literature of the fossil record with regards to the first appearance of megascopic fossil organisms, organisms that are generally called metazoans (animals) or metaphytes (plants). Megascopic fossils (megafossils) are known from as early as 2.3 billion years ago and some of these might be fossils that were made from organisms containing eukaryotic cells. Some prokaryotic organisms can also form megascopic multicelled masses, such as *Nostoc*, a globular mass of cyanobacteria, but most prokaryotic lifeforms are microscopic, and only when vast quantities of prokaryotic cells grow together, do they produce a megascopic structure like a stromatolite.

Distinguishing whether a megafossil was originally from a mass of prokaryotic cells or from an organism composed of eukaryotic cells is very difficult to determine and is problematic. Rarely, as in the case with the Gunflint stromatolites, are the cells of the organisms that formed the stromatolite preserved. Complex morphology in a megafossil is used to distinguish a eukaryotic organism, simple, globular shaped fossils are suggestive of a prokaryotic one; a very subjective distinction indeed.

Three categories of non-stromatolite megafossils exist in most of the Proterozoic. The first consists of what appear to be fossil tracks and trackways (Figs. 06-03 and 06-04); the second consists of elongate, thread or band-like compression fossils (Figs. 06-05 and 06-06); and the third consists of more or less globular or circular (medusiform) fossils, many of which fall under the category of moranids (Figs. 06-07 and 06-08).

Fossil tracks and trackway occurrences are a problem in themselves; tracks and trackways indicate motility and animals are the lifeforms associated with such. Some track-like fossils do occur in very ancient rocks and other than their being considered pseudofossils, their occurrence is puzzling as to what they represent.

Morphologically complex fossils that have a consistent shape, such as *Grypania* (Figure 4), have been attributed, because of their relative complexity, to having been composed of eukaryotic cells, and hence would be plants. Moranids are usually elliptical or globular compressions that can vary in shape and size; they are considered to be aggregates of prokaryotic cells. Moranids can locally occur in great numbers; Proterozoic coal occurs at a few localities in the world and appears to have been made up of vast quantities of moranids. Fragments of moranids have also been confused with parts of animal megafossils, some of which were considered by C. D. Walcott to be fragments of eurypterids, a scorpion-like arthropod (see Chapter 7). Many other Precambrian fossils have been confused with and compared to fossils of the Phanerozoic or with parts of Phanerozoic animals, and these have often turned out to be fragments of moranids.

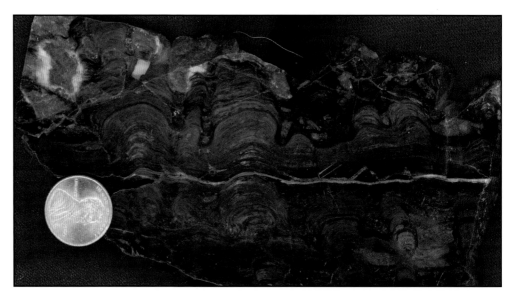

Fig. 06-01. Polished slice of a distinctive and well-formed stromatolite of the form genus *Kussiella* sp. Gunflint Chert, Nolalu, western Ontario. (Value range F)

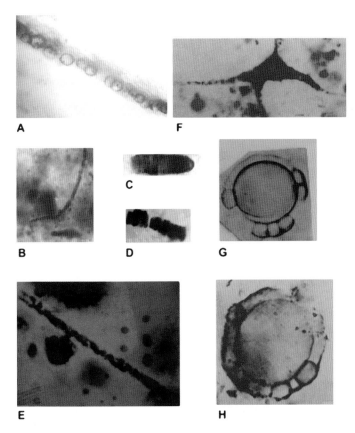

Fig. 06-02. Microfossils from black, flinty beds of the Gunflint Chert near Thunder Bay, Ontario. These small, microscopic organisms have been sealed in silica in a manner similar to that of insects sealed and preserved in amber. A) filament with cells? (circular structures); B) Vague filament of a type seen frequently in thin sections of Gunflint stromatolites; C, D) filaments; E) straight filament; F) Acritarch, a type of microfossil characteristic of the Proterozoic but rare in Gunflint chert; G, H) *Eosphaera* sp., a distinctive microfossil characteristic of the Gunflint and Biwabik formations.

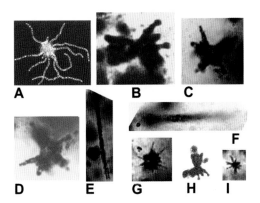

Fig. 06-03. Microfossils associated with black, organic rich chert of the Gunflint Formation, Nolalu, Ontario. A) Drawing of *Kakabekia* sp.; B-D, G-I) *Kakabekia* sp. as photographed through a microscope. These and filaments (E, F) are the most frequently microfossils seen in Gunflint Chert. *Kakabekia* is not directly associated with stromatolites, the filaments are.

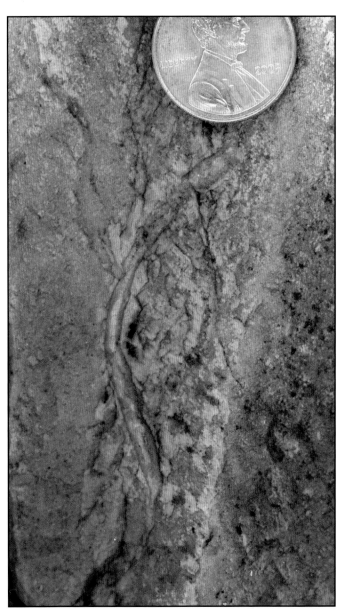

Fig. 06-04. Fossils like this from early Proterozoic rocks of the Canadian Shield have been described as being worm tracks, which they resemble. Considerable confusion exists in the literature on the Precambrian regarding fossils such as these. Some are now explained as sediment filled cracks that developed in a moneran mat on the sea floor. It's a type of fossil all right (even a trace fossil), but not from a worm-like animal—rather, it is from the filling of cracks in a mat produced by monerans. Lorrain Formation, Flack Lake, central Ontario.

Fig. 06-05. *Grypania spiralis*. These spiral fossils, preserved as compressions or carbonaceous films on bedding planes of slaty shale, are one of the oldest suspects for eukaryotic life. Eukaryotic cells contrast strongly with those of prokaryotic life forms; the division between these two forms of life is the most profound one in biology. *Grypania* is the oldest serious candidate for the much more complicated eukaryotic-cell based life form. Negaunee Iron-Formation, Marquette, Michigan. (Value range F)

Fig. 06-07. Moranids. These impressions of "football shaped" colonies of cyanobacteria can be found locally in considerable abundance in Paleoproterozoic black shales. They even can form, by great concentrations of them, coal-like beds. They are also known as graphitic compressions and are suggestive of *Nostoc* sp., a genus of modern cyanobacteria that forms gelatinous blobs on the bottom of streams and lakes. Attikamagen Formation, Schefferville, northern Quebec. (Value range G)

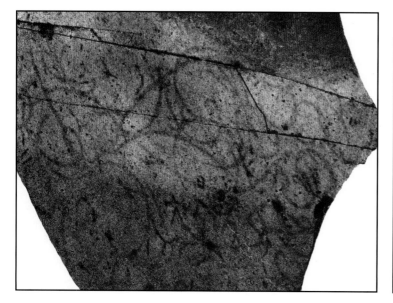

Fig. 06-06. Another iron-rich shale slab with concentrations of *Grypania spiralis*. These fossils somewhat resemble graptolites of the early part of the Paleozoic Era. Graptolites are hemichordates, relatives to the vertebrates. *Grypania* may be a plant or it may represent some sort of unsuccessful prokaryotic evolutionary "experiment." (Value range F)

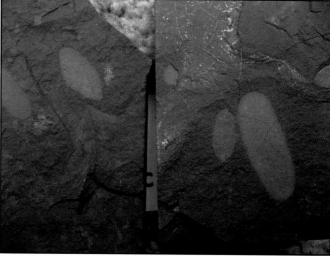

Fig. 06-08. Another group of moranids from the early Proterozoic of the Labrador Trough of northern Quebec.

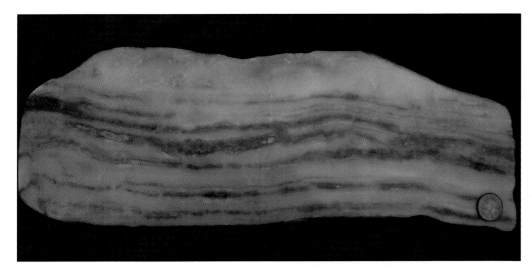

Fig. 06-09. Bad River metamorphosed stromatolites. These laminar stromatolites have been subjected to deep burial and its consequent metamorphism. They are found in beds of marble where impurities, trapped by the mucilage of the original blue-green algae, have been converted by metamorphism to the green mineral epidote, a green silicate mineral. Early Proterozoic, Bad River Formation, Blaylock Wisconsin. (Value range D)

The earliest Proterozoic stromatolites are often similar to those of the Archean, however they occur, on a worldwide basis, more frequently that do the stromatolites of the Archean. In part, this is because the continents began to exist in the Proterozoic and shallow water of continental shelves offered a favorable environment for the growth of stromatolites and colonies of cyanobacteria. Paleoproterozoic strata, like that of the Archean, is often metamorphosed, sometimes highly so. Stromatolites in these metamorphosed sequences are found in marble, and while little detailed structure is preserved, they can be quite attractive.

Fig. 06-10. Outcrop of broad domal stromatolites in the Medicine Bow Mountains, south central Wyoming. Nash Fork Limestone, early Proterozoic.

Fig. 06-11. Another exposure in the Medicine Bow Mountains, of the same zone of stromatolites as in the previous picture.

Fig. 06-12. *Cryptozoon* sp. A slice through a typical *Cryptozoon* "colony." *Cryptozoon* was originally described from Cambrian strata in upstate New York in the mid nineteenth century. Its name means hidden animal, and it was originally thought to be a type of giant rhizopod or protist. The red iron pigment in these specimens suggests its Precambrian age, otherwise it is nearly identical to *Cryptozoon* found in the early Paleozoic. (Value range G)

Fig. 06-13. Wavy, stromatolitic layers, Medicine Bow Mts. The inflection of the layers of this laminar stromatolite is not the signature of a true stromatolite. The structure is a stromatolite (a laminar one), but the bending of the layers came after the moneran mat was deposited. Such folding may be from compression of the mat before it lithified or it might have formed after the moneran mat was incorporated in rock strata. (Value range F)

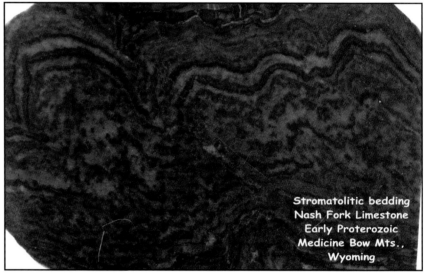

Fig. 06-14. Medium sized domal stromatolites from the same beds as shown in previous picture. The "bending" here is that of a real stromatolite. It formed as a consequence of sediment precipitated on the algal filaments and also from sediment stuck to the mucilaginous material that covers a growing stromatolite and makes it slimy. Stromatolites have a recognizable signature that defies easy description but is readily recognizable, once one becomes familiar with it. Nash Fork Limestone, Medicine Bow Group, Wyoming. (Value range E)

Fig. 06-15. Stromatolite or stromatolitic limestone from the Medicine Bow Mts. cemented into a wall, Centennial Wyoming.

Trace Fossils, Burrows, and Confusion: The Earliest Metazoan Trace Fossils

The definition of a trace fossil is "recognizable evidence of the life activities of some type of organism." Fossil tracks and trackways made by animals such as trilobites, mammals, dinosaurs, etc. are what usually comes to mind with mention of a "trace fossil," but stromatolites are also a type of trace fossil. Stromatolites are structures produced by the physiological activities of microorganisms, hence they are a structure that falls under the definition of a trace fossil. In the conventional view of a trace fossil being tracks, trails, or burrows of animals, the earliest evidence of such should nail down the earliest evidence of animals, however nowhere in paleontology is there such ambivalence as to what is or is not a true animal trace fossil.

There are lots of pseudofossils and dubiofossils that resemble tracks or trackways and hence many "false alarms." Distinguishing real animal trace fossils from false ones can be very difficult and subjective. Some "trace fossils" occur in rock strata of deep time such as the Paleoproterozoic and are serious contenders for evidence of the first animals or at least evidence for large organisms that may or may not have been animals. (Is there a possibility that organismic mobility evolved in some way through "clumping" of prokaryotic cells in a way similar to those of sponges in an evolutionary experiment?) Prokaryotic cells such as bacteria, can have, at the cell posterior, what are called flagella (little whips). Could such cells with their moving flagella have aggregated together in some way to produce a megascopic, motile organism? Early "trace fossils" are ambiguous and difficult to interpret.

There are even reports of fossil burrows in the Archean, however few of these have been taken seriously by paleontologists. The earliest tracks and burrow-like fossils of serious concern occur in the Paleoproterozoic.

One of the more recent and accessible accounts of early Proterozoic trace fossils are occurrences in quartzite of the Medicine Bow Mountains of Wyoming. "Are These the Oldest Trace Fossils?" *Journal of Paleontology*, 1981 addresses the question of the earliest occurrences of Precambrian trace fossils. These Medicine Bow Mountains "trace fossils" exemplify the problem of distinguishing those structures actually made by a moving organism from those made by some other, non-living process.

One frequently occurring rock type of the Paleoproterozoic is iron formation. Believed to be a rock record of the transition of the earth's atmosphere from an aerobic one to an anoxic one, iron formation occurred as a consequence of precipitation of iron oxide from the presence of photosynthetically produced oxygen. Proterozoic iron formation sometimes contains beautiful stromatolites, like those found in the Biwabik Iron Formation of northern Minnesota or its equivalent, the Gunflint Formation of western Ontario. These iron formations, particularly when they are weathered, produce much of the commercial iron ore of North America as well as in Australia.

The Medicine Bow Mountains quartzite does yield undoubted fossils that can easily be confused with burrows (Figs. 05-16 and 05-18). These fossils come in the a form of narrow, elongate and closely spaced digitate stromatolites of the form genus *Conophyton* sp. Such stromatolites resemble the trace fossil *Skolithus* sp., a vertical burrow that appears in abundance at the very beginning of the Cambrian Period or at the very end of the Neoproterozoic. Other burrow-like trace fossils are found in the mesoproterozoic, where problematic fossils, possibly produced by assemblages of prokaryotes, are also found.

Fig. 06-16 and 06-17. Foolers—are these trace fossils? They look like vertical "burrows," sliced vary thin and seen by transmitted light, and are somewhat similar to *Scolithus* or *Skolithos*, a vertical worm burrow common in some sandstones of Phanerozoic age. They are from Paleoproterozoic sandstone (now quartzite), of the Medicine Bow Mountains of Wyoming. They are not animal trace fossils but are very narrow, digitate stromatolites of the form genus *Conophyton*. *Conophyton* is often associated with cyanobacteria growing in hot springs or other geothermal areas. These stromatolites have been sliced very thin and backlighted to bring out the skolithos-like structure. Structures similar to these have been described from these same quartzites in "Are These the Earliest Known Trace Fossils?" *Journal of Paleontology*, 1981. Early Proterozoic, Medicine Bow Mts., Wyoming. (Value range F)

Fig. 06-18. This domal stromatolite comes from a sequence of colorful and very attractive stromatolite reefs near Marquette, Michigan. These stromatolites are cut and polished by rockhounds into a variety of objects. Kona Dolomite, Early Proterozoic, Marquette Michigan. (Value range G)

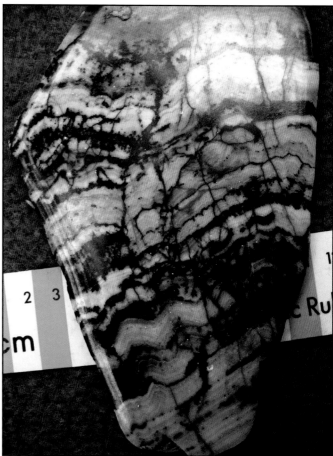

Fig. 06-20. Laminar, iron rich Kona Dolomite stromatolite. A number of different variants of Kona Dolomite stromatolites can be found on the fossil market. Specimens like this (usually slabs) have been widely distributed among collectors. (Value range G)

Fig. 06-19. Another variant on Kona Dolomite stromatolites. This is a laminar stromatolite, quite attractive. The Kona Dolomite and its stromatolites probably correlate with the Bad River Marble of Wisconsin, a source of the metamorphosed, epidote replaced stromatolites, pictured in Fig. 06-09. (Value range H)

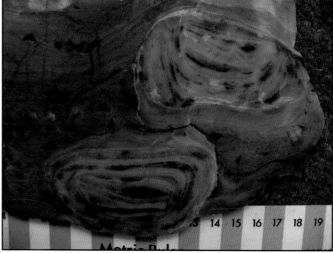

Fig. 06-21. Oncolites, Kona Dolomite. Kona Dolomite stromatolites are readily available, these oncolites less so. Oncolites are another type of cyanobacterial structure. Unlike stromatolites, however, they are not attached to a substrate. With oncolites, the layers of mineral matter are precipitated around some sort of nucleus and build up concentrically around that nucleus. Marquette, Michigan. (Value range E)

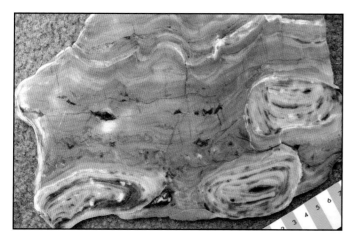

Fig. 06-22. Another cluster of oncolites from the Kona Dolomite of Marquette, Michigan. (Value range E)

Fig. 06-24. *Pilbara perplexa*. Duck Creek Dolomite, Western Australia. This lateral slice of a digitate stromatolite comes from early Proterozoic strata that overlies Archean rocks of the Pilbara Block, Ashburton Trough or basin, Western Australia. (Value range E)

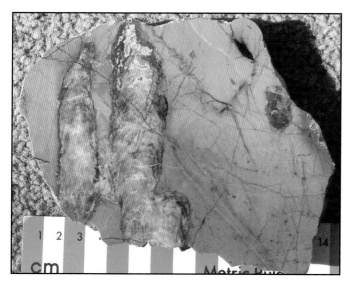

Fig. 06-23. *Pilbaria perplexa*. This digitate stromatolite comes from strata at the edge of the Pilbara Block, part of the oldest geologic terraine in Australia. Part of the Pilbara Block yields the oldest known stromatolites (see Fig. 05-19) from Archean strata that underlies the Proterozoic strata from which these stromatolites were collected. This digitate stromatolite, from the Duck Creek Dolomite, has been given the form genus Pilbaria and species perplexa. Some geologists concur with giving distinctive stromatolites like this a binomial even though a stromatolite is a structure produced by a group of organisms rather than having been an individual organism. Others prefer to refer to stromatolites ino general terms such as digitate, domal, laminar, or to express their morphology be the use of a formula. Early Proterozoic, Duck Creek Dolomite, Ashburton Trough or basin, Western Australia. (Value range E)

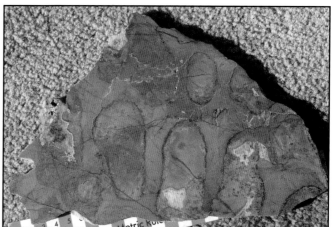

Fig. 06-25. *Pilbara perplexa*. This is a horizontal slice across the "fingers" of this distinctive stromatolite. Some paleontologists support the concept of giving a distinctive stromatolite such as this a binomial name (form genus and species) on the grounds that each stromatolite occurrence was a distinctive moneran community. Others disagree with this and consider that a stromatolite, being a product of many variables including such physical ones as water depth and salinity, latitude of growth, tidal action etc., in addition to their biogenic makeup, is a physical structure as much as a biogenic one and as such a binomial name is inappropriate. Duck Creek Dolomite, Ashburton Trought or basin, Western Australia, (Value range E)

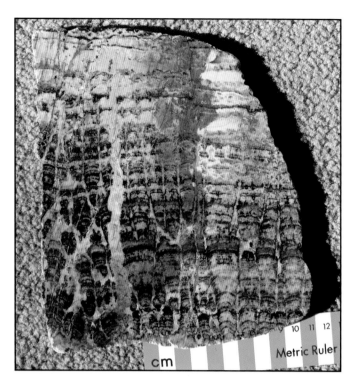

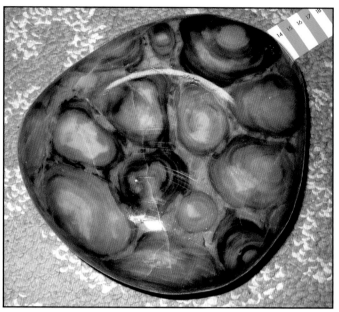

Fig. 06-28. Talc stromatolites. Talc is a metamorphic mineral and one not normally associated with fossils! This is an example of peculiar preservation of stromatolite structure associated with Precambrian strata of Western Australia. This group of *Kussiella*-like or *Collenia* sp. stromatolites in talc have had their original limestone or dolomite composition altered to this material from hydrothermal alteration associated with a nearby igneous (dolerite) intrusion. This specimen shows top (plan) view of a cluster of stromatolites. From talc mine near Three Springs, Western Australia, Coomberdale Subgroup, "Noondine Chert" (Value range D)

Fig. 06-26. *Asperia ashburtonia*. This columnar-layered stromatolite is almost identical with late Archean forms from the Yellowknife Supergroup of NWT Canada as well as ones from the Archean Bulawayan Greenstone Belt, Zimbabwe, Africa. This specimen comes from the early Proterozoic Duck Creek Dolomite of Western Australia. It is debated as to whether stromatolites like these can be used as indexes to the age of Precambrian strata and that some stromatolite types even changed over long spans of geologic time. This type of columnar-layered strom does appear to be characteristic of the early Precambrian. From Duck Creek Dolomite, Ashburton Trought or basin, Western Australia. (Value range E)

Fig. 06-29. Open pit iron mine in weathered paleoproterozoic Biwabik Iron Formation, northern Minnesota. The iron mines of northern Minnesota, in the Mesabi Iron Range, are the source of much of the iron ore used in steel making in North America. Such iron, concentrated in the ores of the mines, originally came from iron dissolved in bodies of water 2.1 billion years ago and precipitated by biogenic activity associated with photosynthesis.

Fig. 06-27. *Asperia ashburtonia*. Close-up of cut slab of this distinctive columnar-layered stromatolite. These closely packed strom columns are suggested to have grown under conditions where they were subjected to intermittent periods of submergence and emergence, possibly from very high seasonal tides. It is suggested by astronomers that in the early history of the earth, the moon was closer to the earth than it is today with proportionally greater tides. This type of stromatolite is characteristic of the early rock record of the earth and might be a consequence of this hypothesis. Duck Creek Dolomite, Wyloo Group, Pilbara region, Western Australia. (Value range E)

Fig. 06-32. Biwabik stromatolites come in a variety of shades and colors; all are attractive. This specimen is dark from a lot of iron oxide. Attractive and varied specimens of Biwabik stromatolites have been distributed in the fossil market as some of the oldest fossils. (Value range G)

Fig. 06-30. *Gymnosolen* sp., also often labeled as *Collenia undosa*. The stromatolites of the Biwabik iron formation represent tangible evidence of vast concentrations of cyanobacterial colonies precipitating iron to form iron-rich sediments which, upon weathering, had their iron concentrated into minable iron ore. This distinct fossil of the stromatolite genus *Gymnsolen* has been widely distributed by the fossil market, most of the specimens having come from iron mines of the Mesabi Iron Range of Minnesota. (Value range F)

Fig. 06-33. A horizontal slice across the "fingers" of a Biwabik digitate stromatolite. Individual fingers, when sliced, produce circular or concentric rings. Biwabik Iron Formation, northern Minnesota. (Value range F)

Fig. 06-31. *Collenia undosa* or *Gymnosolen*. Part of a slice through a mass of digitate stromatolites. Known to rockhounds as Mary Ellen jasper, this beautiful stromatolite comes from the Biwabik Iron Formation of Northern Minnesota. The iron formation in which it occurs forms part of the iron deposits in that part of the Canadian Shield. The Biwabik is equivalent to the Gunflint Formation across the border in western Ontario. The Gunflint has yielded a variety of microfossils associated with its stromatolites and it was the presence of these microfossils which convinced geologists that very ancient stromatolites in the rock record were indeed of biogenic origin. (Value range F)

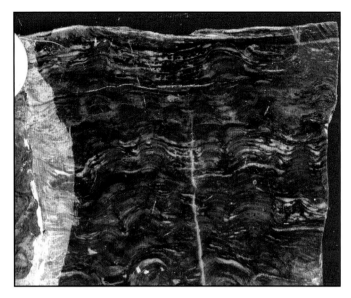

Fig. 06-34. *Stratiferia biwabikensis* A distinctive type of laminar stromatolite from the Biwabik Iron Formation. Colorful specimens, some with green pigments, have come onto the fossil market recently from iron mines of northern Minnesota. This specimen has been altered by the intrusion of a granite mass that has "cooked" the stromatolite bearing horizon, producing dark colors. Magnetic Trail, Northern Minnesota. (Value range G)

Fig. 06-35. "*Collenia undosa*" or *Kussiella superiora*. Bifurcating stromatolitic fingers like this are also referred to as the form genus *Gymnosolen*. If a large part of a stromatolite reef can be seen in one outcrop, extensive branching is often seen. The part of the reef from which a hand specimen has come will determine the name used. Genera such as *Kussiella, Conophyton,* and *Collenia* refer to specific parts of a larger stromatolite reef. The form genera *Jucutophyton, Baicalia. Yungussia* and *Boxonia* are form genera that apply to an entire stromatolite reef complex. Biwabik Iron Formation. Paleoproterozoic. (Value range F)

Fig. 06-36. Left half of slab with broad fingers of *Kussiella* sp., narrow "finger" between them. Black material in upper right where fingers are absent is anthroxolite. Gunflint Chert, Nolalu, Ontario. (Value range G)

Fig. 06-37. Digitate (finger-like) stromatolites from the 2.2 billion year old Gunflint Formation of western Ontario, Canada. Microfossils associated with these stromatolites proved beyond doubt the biogenicity of many ancient viz. early Precambrian stromatolites. Prior to this discovery, many paleontologists questioned the biogenic origin of numerous early stromatolites because they occurred in rock strata that was so much more ancient than strata that yielded most other fossils.

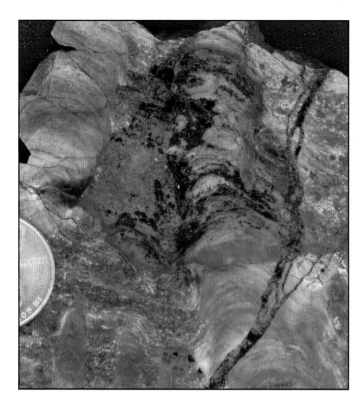

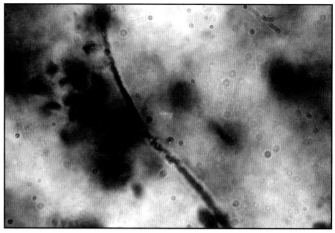

Fig. 06-40. Gunflint cyanobacterial filament. Typical fossil filament associated with Gunflint stromatolite, Gunflint chert, Nolalu, Ontario.

Fig. 06-38. Slab with *Kussiella superiora*, Gunflint Formation, Paleoproterozoic. Most of the stromatolites from the Biwabik and Gunflint formations are labeled as *Collenia undosa* by collectors and fossil dealers. In fact, there are a number of stromatolite form genera in these strata, often with one form grading into another. *Kussiella* forms straight "fingers" and does not bifurcate. Black material is anthroxolite, a high molecular weight asphaltic hydrocarbon similar to the material in carbonaceous chondrites. Nolalu, Northwestern Ontario, Canada. (Value range G)

Fig. 06-41. Biwabik stromatolites containing large amounts of hematite. The occurrence of digitate stromatolites in northern Minnesota is often associated with hematite as in this specimen. Such hematite is probably secondary and is not entirely a product of original cyanobacterial precipitation. Microfossil assemblages like those of the Gunflint Formation to the east are absent from these "stroms," presumably destroyed by oxidization when more hematite was introduced. (Value range G)

Fig. 06-39. A specimen of the peculiar and distinctive microfossil *Kakabekia* sp., from the Gunflint chert near Nolalu, Ontario.

Fig. 06-42. Outcrop of Gunflint chert with the tops of digitate fingers showing. Nolalu, Ontario.

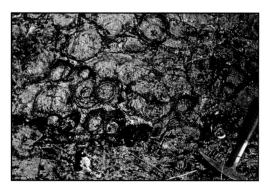

Fig. 06-43. Glaciated surface of stromatolite "colony." Horizontal cross sections of stromatolites are in a white limestone of the Kaniapiskau Supergroup, a complex sequence of early Proterozoic sediments making the Labrador Trough in the northern part of New Quebec (Ungava), Canada.

Fig. 06-44. Another part of the stromatolite "reef" near Otelnuk Lake, Labrador Trough or geosyncline, northern Quebec, Canada. Stromatolite bands have weathered in relief being high in silica. Stromatolite "reefs" like this occur worldwide in early and mid-Proterozoic limestones. From the perspective of a higher life form, the blue-green algae of such a reef represents a gigantic salad that could be cropped and eaten. The fact that such extensive reefs abound in the Proterozoic implies that no such "croppers" had yet come onto the scene, at least not in any large number. Such extensive stromatolite development like this is rare after the lowest and earliest part of the Ordovician Period of the Paleozoic Era.

Fig. 06-45. Laminar stromatolites in white limestones of the Labrador Trough. Limestone beds of this early Proterozoic sequence are full of stromatolites, many of which are similar to stromatolites of the same age found in Africa, particularly sub-Saharan Africa.

Fig. 06-46. Top portions of some of the stromatolites of the reefs shown in Figs. 06-43 and 06-44. Some of the patterns seen here are suggestive of the stromatoporoids of the Paleozoic Era. White limestone of the Kaniapiskau Supergroup, Otelnuk Lake, Northern Quebec.

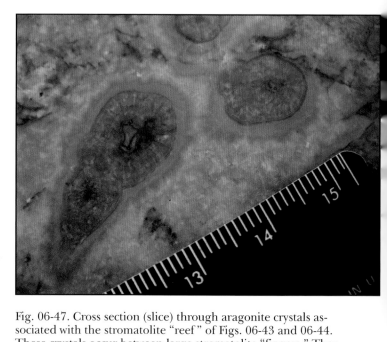

Fig. 06-47. Cross section (slice) through aragonite crystals associated with the stromatolite "reef" of Figs. 06-43 and 06-44. These crystals occur between large stromatolite "fingers." They probably represent crystal fillings between the stromatolite domes or "fingers" but their intimate placement between stroms hints of biogenicity. They are problematic like so many Precambrian biogenic-like structures and would best be placed under the category of dubiofossils. Otelnuk Lake, Labrador Trough.

Fig. 06-48. Slice through a single elongate dome of *Kussiella* sp., red limestone sequence, Otelnuk Lake, northern Quebec. These stromatolites, in red, iron-rich limestone occur in a different part of the Kaniapiskau Supergroup of the Labrador Trough than do the stromatolite reefs of the previous images. Similar stromatolites, in red limestone occur in slightly younger beds of Montana and China where the Chinese quarry and cut them for use as decorative stone in buildings. (Value range G)

Fig. 06-50. *Anomolophycus* sp. A distinctive form genus of stromatolite from red limestones of the Kaniapiskau Supergroup, Otelnuk Lake, northern Quebec.

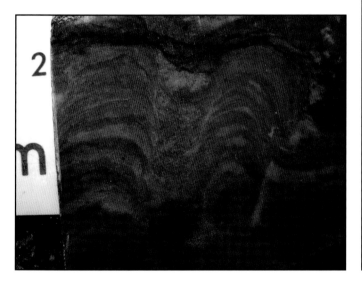

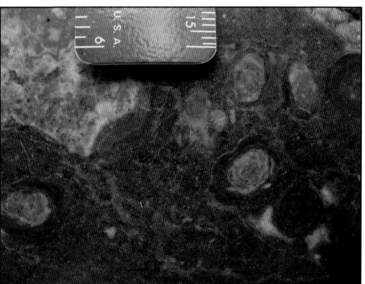

Fig. 06-49. *Collenia* sp. A similar specimen as in the previous image, from the same red limestone sequence of the Labrador Trough or geosyncline. Here two stromatolitic "fingers" are present. Otelnuk Lake, northern Quebec. (Value range for similar material G)

Fig. 06-51. Group of oncolites, red limestone sequence, Kaniapiskau Supergroup, Otelnuk Lake. Oncolites are concretionary structures produced by mineral build-up from a community of monerans. They sometimes occur at the margins of stromatolite reefs associated with higher energy waters. They can still be found today associated with the surf zone of coral reefs and are sometimes called sea biscuits. Geologically recent and modern oncolites are not always so nicely rounded in shape, often being nibbled on and cropped by higher life forms—higher life forms that did not yet exist when these oncolites were formed. (Value range for a slab of similar material of similar age G.)

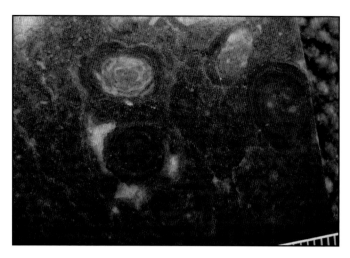

Fig. 06-52. Another group of oncolites from the Labrador Trough, red limestone sequence. Some modern oncolites are made by the cyanobacteria *Spirogyra* sp. This can be purchased in health food stores and, according to some, makes a tasty, healthful treat. Otelnuk Lake, northern Quebec. These oncolites are similar in shape and age to those in Figs. 06-21 and 06-22 from the Kona Dolomite of northern Michigan. (Value range of similar material G)

Fig. 06-54. More foolers. If these worm-track-like fossils were found in Phanerozoic strata, they would not be questioned as to their origin from crawling worms. But in the early Proterozoic such organisms should not have existed. They may have been made by portions of algal mats moving along the sea floor. Otelnuk Lake, northern Quebec.

Fig. 06-53. Foolers! If these were found on a bedding surface of Phanerozoic rock, they would be unremarkable "fossil worm tracks." However, it's from 2.2 billion year old strata from western Ontario! If this were a real worm track, it would mean that animals had been around three times longer than the Cambrian fossil record shows. In addition, **worms**, being made up of **eukaryotic** cells, would indicate that these more complex cell-types were also around that early. Fossils like these, found in very ancient rock strata, have fooled paleontologists for decades. In reality, this is the sediment filling of a crack formed by desiccation of a moneran mat. Drying associated with a layer of cyanobacteria or bacteria can produce animal-like fossils like this. This discovery has explained many, but not all, of the very ancient, early Precambrian (Paleoproterozoic) trace fossils. Desiccation cracks, produced by shrinkage of a moneran mat, which was then covered with sand, made these patterns. Isolated, sediment-filled shrinkage cracks can resemble animal tracks or even parts of animals. These seem to be the source of many of the reported "animal fossils" in Precambrian strata. Bar River Formation, Paleoproterozoic, western Ontario.

Fig. 06-55. Another view of mid-Precambrian worm-like-track dubiofossils. Otelnuk Lake, northern Quebec.

Fig. 06-56. Archean or Paleoproterozoic iron formation. Sometimes early Proterozoic rocks and fossils are noted as Archean. This is because of variances in numerical values (decay constants) used in radiometric age dates.

Fig. 06-57. Hematite rich stromatolite possibly produced by colonies of chemosynthetic bacteria. These small hematite "bursts" are associated with a thin iron formation bed, which may have had its origin as small colonies of either photosynthetic or chemosynthetic bacteria. Many stromatolite-like structures like these, sometimes containing metallic oxides, occur in the early rock record. Many earth scientists refuse to acknowledge a biogenic origin for these; in consideration of them, however, it should be kept in mind that life of the early earth was probably just as opportunistic as it is today, so any suitable environment would have provided a medium for growth of some type of moneran. From strata at the bottom of the Belt Series near Niehart, Montana. (Value range G)

Bibliography

Barghoorn, Elso S., and S. M. Tyler. "Microfossils from the Gunflint Chert." *Science* 147: No. 3658, 1965, pg. 563-577.

Cloud, Preston. "The significance of the Gunflint (Precambrian) microflora." *Science* Vol. 148, 1965, pg. 27-35.

Gould, Stephen J. "An Unsung Single-Celled Hero," in *Ever Since Darwin: Reflections on Natural History*. New York, N.Y.: W. W. Norton Company, 1977.

Hofmann, Hans J. "Precambrian Fossils. Pseudofossils and Problematica in Canada." *Geological Survey of Canada*, Bulletin 189, 1971.

Kaufmann, Earl. "Are These the Earliest Trace Fossils?" *Journal of Paleontology*, Volume 55, No. 5, 1981, pg. 923-947.

Knoll, Andrew H. *Life on a Young Planet: The First Three Billion Years of Evolution on Earth*. Princeton, New Jersey: Princeton University Press, 2003.

Schopf, J. W. *The Proterozoic Biosphere: A Multidisciplinary Study*. Cambridge: Cambridge University Press, 1992.

Tsu-Ming and Bruce Runnegar. "Megascopic Eukaryotic Algae from 2.1 Billion Year Old Negaunee Iron Formation, Michigan." *Science*, Vol. 257, 1992, pp. 232-235.

"Treatise on Invertebrate Paleontology." Part W. *Miscellanea, Supplement 1, Trace Fossils and Problematica, 2nd Edition*. The Geological Society of America and University of Kansas, 1975.

Chapter Seven
The Mesoproterozoic

Mesoproterozoic rock strata is often not so deformed and metamorphosed as is strata of the Paleoproterozoic. Stromatolites in the mesoproterozoic are more likely to be present than in older strata, and during this time they probably reached their greatest diversity in the history of the earth, often forming large and complex structures. Mesoproterozoic stroms can also be quite attractive and colorful, as iron salts giving reds, pinks, and greens had not yet been totally flushed from the waters of the world's oceans, and these were often incorporated into the stromatolite when it was forming. In more regions than is the case with earlier strata, that of the Mesoproterozoic age sometimes has its beds still in the horizontal position in which they were originally laid down.

Prokaryotic life, as represented by various forms of stromatolites, was still the dominant form of life in the Mesoproterozoic, however what are interpreted as early eukaryotic organisms have been reported and some fossils of the Mesoproterozoic are considered to have been made by organisms with eukaryotic cell types. Determining whether the cell type of a fossil organism was prokaryotic or eukaryotic is wrought with difficulties, however. Definitive animal trace fossils are still missing, although a number of structures have been reported that suggest movement on the sea floor by some type of organism.

A thick Mesoproterozoic sequence of limestone, now metamorphosed to marble, occurs in the eastern portion of North America, the so-called Grenville Series. Beds of marble in this sequence yield stromatolites, although they are often hard to recognize because of severe metamorphism.

Grenville marbles also yield a number of puzzling structures, including Eozoon canadense, the "dawn animal" of Canada. Archaeospherina is another Grenville pseudofossil, once considered to be the reproductive "buds" of Eozoon.

Flattened graphitic bodies, which are probably from globular bodies similar to those that formed moranids (Fig. 06-07) or *Chuaria* (Fig. 07-64), occur in beds of the marble. These are also similar to *Carelozoon,* one of the "zoons" found in the Precambrian of Finland.

Fig. 07-01. Metamorphosed domal stromatolite in marble. The Mesoproterozoic Grenville marbles of Quebec and upstate New York contain zones of highly crystalline marble that were originally limestone. Vague laminate structures in this marble are almost certainly the outlines of once abundant stromatolites in the original limestone. Iron minerals, present as impurities in the limestone, now give the greenish color of epidote to these structures. Grenville Marble, Adirondack Mts., northern New York. (Value range G)

Fig. 07-02. Grenville marble with graphite crystals. Severe metamorphism has converted organic material in the limestone to the graphite of this very crystalline rock. The carbon in the graphite crystals (black) presumably came from organic carbon originally in the parent limestone and probably from cyanobacteria. (Value range H for similar material)

Fig. 07-03. *Carelozoon* sp. Cut surface of one of the "zoons." *Carelozoon* and a similar dubiofossil, *Corycium enigmatum*, originally were described from Precambrian rocks of Finland. Both of these forms appear to have been formed from what originally were globular organic bodies that are now represented by either flattened graphitic bodies or by graphitic granular bodies in marble. Such algal masses are represented today by cyanobacteria such as the genus *Nostoc* sp., which form gelatinous, globular bodies. Specimens from Finland, that part of Europe with the oldest rocks, are in marble, as are these specimens from the Grenville Series, Maniwaki, Quebec, Canada.

Fig. 07-04. *Carelozoon* sp. Fractured surface across a series of flattened but probably originally globular carbonaceous bodies in Grenville marble. Similar carbonaceous structures are represented by the genus *Chuaria*, a fossil originally described by Charles Walcott from shales of the Grand Canyon and Montana (see Figs. 07-64 and 07-65). Grenville Marble, Maniwaki, Quebec.

Eozoon canadense was the first Precambrian "fossil" to gain notoriety. It is attractive and looks biogenic, particularly on weathered outcrops.

Fig. 07-05. *Cryptozoon* sp.? A horizontal slice through a type of iron-rich stromatolite that forms extensive "reefs" along the north side of Great Slave Lake, NWT Canada. From strata of the same age as Eozoon but a bonafide stromatolite.

Fig. 07-07. *Eozoon canadense* (the "dawn animal" of Canada). Another variant on Eozoon. Whitish band is a crack along which weathering has taken place. Lac Charlebois, Quebec. (Value range F)

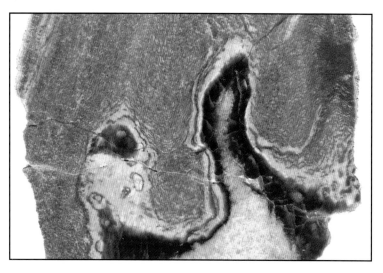

Fig. 07-06. *Eozoon canadense* (the "dawn animal" of Canada). This is a specimen of the famous Eozoon from the original Cote St. Pierre, Quebec locality, north of Ottawa, Ontario, Canada. Eozoon was the first "fossil" described from Precambrian rocks but is now considered as a pseudofossil produced through severe metamorphism of limestone, possibly stromatolitic limestone. Grenville marble, Cote St. Pierre, Quebec.

Fig. 07-08. Slab of Eozoon with diopside nodule (white) surrounded by a thick layer of serpentine. The Eozoon "animal" was considered to have grown on and around the diopside nodule. (Value range G)

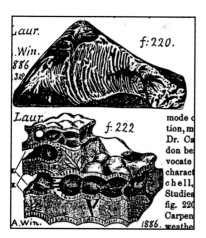

Fig. 07-09. Original figures of Eozoon, illustrating what was considered in the extensive late nineteenth century literature on Eozoon to be biogenically formed microstructure. From J.W. Dawson, *Canadian Naturalist*, Vol. 2, 1865.

Fig. 07-12. *Eozoon* (top) and *Archaeospherina* (bottom of slab); white mineral is calcite. Lac Charlebois, Quebec. (Value range F)

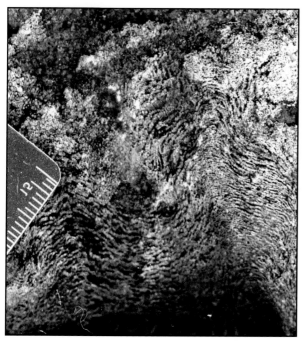

Fig. 07-10. Weathered surface of Eozoon suggesting some similarity to stromatolites, Lac Charlebois, Quebec. (Value range F)

Fig. 07-13. *Eozoon canadense,* Dawson 1864. A slab of the "dawn animal" of Canada. The green mineral is serpentine in a matrix of calcite; at the bottom by the pencil is diopside. *Eozoon* is found in occurrences associated with magma intrusions in 1.5 billion year old marble of the Grenville Series of eastern Ontario and southern Quebec. (Value range G)

Fig. 07-11. Close up of weathered surface of Eozoon, Lac Charlebois, Quebec. (Value range F)

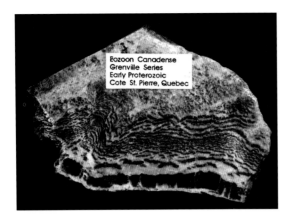

Fig. 07-14. Variant on Eozoon from the Lac Charlebois locality in Quebec. (Value range F)

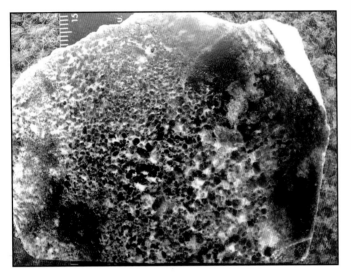

Fig. 07-15. *Archaeospherina* is the original generic name given to these concretionary spherules found in association with *Eozoon canadense*. They were considered by advocates of the biogenicity of *Eozoon* to be the reproductive "buds" or clones of the *Eozoon* "animal." These spherical "buds," like other portions of *Eozoon*, are composed of serpentine, a mineral rarely associated with fossils (but see Fig. 09-56). Laurentian (Grenville) Mesoproterozoic marble, Cote St. Pierre locality, Quebec. (Value range G)

Fig. 07-16. *Archaeospherina* Dawson 1864. A slab of the reproductive "buds" of Eozoon. The green mineral is serpentine in a matrix of calcite. *Eozoon* is found in reef-like occurrences in 1.5 billion year old Laurentian marble beds of the Grenville Series of eastern Ontario and southern Quebec. (Value range G)

A much less metamorphosed Mesoproterozoic sequence occurs on the western side of North America, where it makes up part of the Grand Canyon as well as many of the mountains of the northern Rockies of Montana, Idaho, and Alberta; it is known as the Belt Supergroup. Belt strata consists of a thick sequence made up of hard black and red shales, black and red limestones, and hard mudstones, sometimes with interbedded layers of volcanic lavas or intruded into the sedimentary layers in horizontal beds, called a sill. Stromatolites can be locally abundant in Belt strata and some of these are very strange.

Fig. 07-17. Horizontal section (slice) through a typical mid-Proterozoic stromatolite. Siyeh Limestone, Belt Supergroup, Essex, Montana. (Value range F)

Fig. 07-18. A domal stromatolite of the form genus *Malacostroma* sp. from near Essex, Montana. The signature of the lamina as seen here is typical of the texture of stromatolites made of the cyanobacteria genus *Oscillatoria* sp. Altyn Limestone, Belt Supergroup, mid-Proterozoic. (Value range F)

Fig. 07-19. *Collenia* sp. A weathered surface of a classic Belt stromatolite. The Belt Supergroup of Western Montana, Idaho, and British Columbia contains a variety of often large and spectacular stromatolites as well as a variety of other puzzling structures, which, like stromatolites, form reef-like structures in the Belt sediments. (Value range F)

Fig. 07-20. Impressions of a series of small, domal stromatolites forming an algal mat. This pattern is typical of small stromatolites incorporated into an algal mat. It grew on a sandy substrate that is now pink quartzite. Belt Supergroup, Helena, Montana. (Value range E)

Fig. 07-21. Weathered surface of a Belt stromatolite, *Collenia* sp. Often these contain iron oxide that was removed from sea water through the presence of free oxygen generated by photosynthesis of the cyanobacteria, which produced the stromatolite. Dissolved ferrous iron had to be removed from the world's oceans by this process before free or elemental oxygen could accumulate to form a major portion of the earth's atmosphere. (Value range F)

Fig. 07-22. Domal stromatolites of the form genus *Kussiella*. West of White Sulphur Springs, Montana. Newland Limestone, Belt Supergroup. (Value range F)

Fig. 07-25. *Collenia* sp. Altyn Limestone, Essex, Montana. Well-formed stromatolites occur in boulders along creeks draining into the Flathead River and in the river itself south of Glacier Park. They are associated with a black, almost petroliferous Neoproterozoic limestone of the Belt Supergroup. These stromatolites are found resting on a lower siltstone layer that lacks the organic material. (Value range F)

Fig. 07-23. Close-up of same specimen as in previous photo.

Fig. 07-26. Stromatolite from the Siyeh Limestone of the Belt Supergroup, Kalispell, Montana. The greenish layer at the bottom represents unoxidized sediments with ferrous iron. The red of the stromatolite represents ferric iron, oxidized by free or elemental oxygen generated by photosynthesis of the stromatolites cyanobacteria. This is a fossil record of the early stages of the formation of an oxidizing atmosphere on the earth. (Value range F)

Fig. 07-24. Domal stromatolite completely removed from white limestone of the Belt Supergroup. Reefs of stromatolite domes like these characterized shallow and clear water areas that covered parts of Montana, Alberta, and British Columbia in the mid or Mesoproterozoic. Siyeh Limestone, Belt Supergroup, Kalispell, Montana. (Value range F)

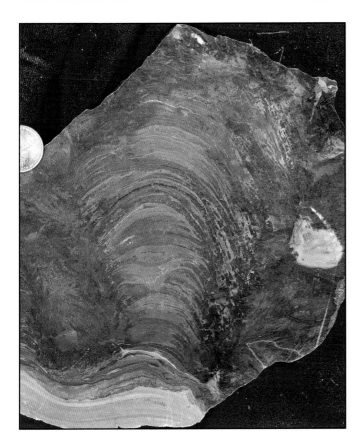

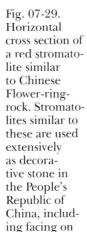

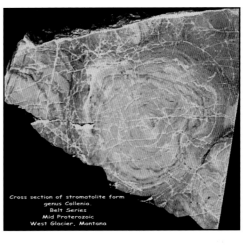

Fig. 07-29. Horizontal cross section of a red stromatolite similar to Chinese Flower-ring-rock. Stromatolites similar to these are used extensively as decorative stone in the People's Republic of China, including facing on the buildings around Tiannamen Square. Slabs of a large, mid-Proterozoic stromatolite "reef" are quarried and cut into tiles, where the stromatolites make a pleasing pattern. Siyeh Limestone, Kalispell, Montana. (Value range G)

Fig. 07-27. *Collenia* sp. Black limestone of the Altyn Limestone, Essex, Montana. These well proportioned stromatolites contain a considerable amount of organic matter that is from the original cyanobacteria and possibly other monerans responsible for the stromatolites. Some of the limestones containing the stromatolites, and particularly the stromatolites themselves, give off a slight petroliferous smell when freshly broken from contained mid-Proterozoic petroleum. (Value range F)

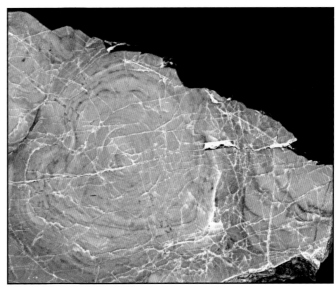

Fig. 07-30. Another Flower-ring-rock stromatolite from the Siyeh Limestone, Belt Supergroup, Kalispell, Montana.

Fig. 07-28. A variant on Belt stromatolites. These nice domes from the Siyeh Limestone of the Belt Supergroup form stromatolite "reefs," which are well exposed at places in Glacier National Park as well as south of the park. Similar specimen as in Fig. 07-25.

Fig. 07-31. Complex stromatolite that has grown on a limestone pebble or clast. Siyeh Limestone, Kalispell, Montana. (Value range F)

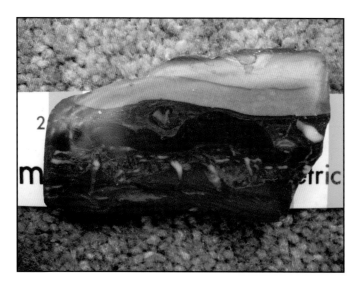

Fig. 07-32. Bacterial stromatolite, Ravalli, Montana. Slightly laminated stromatolites forming "buttons" or knobs on the sea floor like these are attributed to having been made by photosynthetic bacteria rather than cyanobacteria. They may also have been associated with or grew near geothermal sources that supplied the sulfur disseminated as pyrite through the structure. Ravalli Formation, Belt Supergroup, Ravalli, Montana. (Value range F)

Fig. 07-33. Similar specimen of a bacterial stromatolite as in previous photo. Ravalli Group, Ravalli, Montana.

Fig. 07-34. *Collenia* sp. A small domal stromatolite from near the top of the Belt Supergroup, Western Alberta. The Belt group or its equivalents extend northward into Yukon Territory, Canada and southward to the Grand Canyon.

Mesoproterozoic strata similar to the Belt Supergroup crop out in other parts of the world, including Russia, Australia, Namibia, and Morocco.

Fig. 07-35. *Collenia* sp. Mesoproterozoic, High Atlas Mountains, Morocco. Specimens of these distinctive iron rich stromatolites from an undetermined locality in the Atlas Mountains of Morocco have been distributed to the fossil-phile community of Europe and North America through the Tucson, Arizona show. (Value range F)

A 1.8 billion year old volcanic sequence occurs in the southern part of the Canadian shield in Minnesota, and similar strata 1.5 billion years old occur at the center of the Ozark Uplift of Missouri. The Missouri occurrence includes distinctive laminar stromatolites apparently formed in shallow lakes surrounded by or containing hot springs.

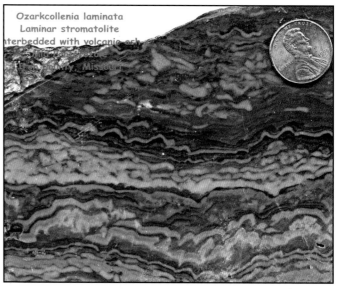

Fig. 07-36. Slice through a laminar stromatolite interbedded with beds of volcanic ash. *Ozarkcollenia* is the form genus of this distinctive stromatolite. A similar stromatolite from Australia, given the form genus *Alcheringa*, is associated with similar volcanic ash beds of the same age. Slabs of *Ozarkcollenia* have been distributed through the fossil-phile community. Cuthbertson Mountain, Iron County, Missouri (Value range F)

Fig. 07-37. A slab of *Ozarkcollenia laminata*, a laminar stromatolite from the mid-Proterozoic of the Ozark Uplift of Missouri. The pinkish layers represent iron and manganese rich material deposited by filamentous cyanobacteria. The algal mats were periodically blanketed by falls of volcanic ash but would re-establish themselves as a new mat after each fall of volcanic ash. (Value range F)

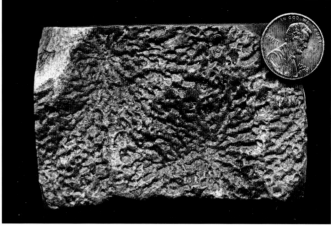

Fig. 07-40. Impression of small stromatolite domes of *Ozarkcollenia* in a slab of volcanic tuff. Volcanic ash, falling upon a surface of a group of stromatolites, left this impression of the stromatolite and algal mat. Ketcherside tuffs, Iron County, Missouri. (Value range F)

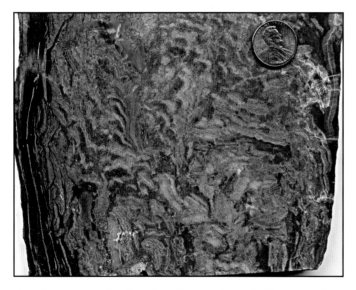

Fig. 07-38. Somewhat "confused" mass of *Ozarkcollenia* associated with beds of volcanic ash (tuff). Ketcherside tuffs, Cuthbertson Mountain, Iron County, Missouri (Value range F)

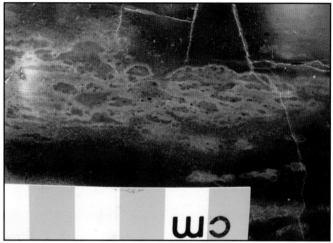

Fig. 07-41. Small domes and mat of stromatolites in volcanic tuff that have been converted by metamorphism to the green silicate mineral epidote. Pressure and chemical changes associated with relatively deep burial of the volcanic tuffs that covered the stromatolite changed the calcium carbonate of the stromatolite into epidote. Iron from the surrounding tuff was incorporated into the stromatolite, forming a lighter iron free "halo" around each stromatolite dome. Cope Hollow Formation, Reynolds County, Missouri (Value range G)

Fig. 07-39. Three slabs of *Ozarkcollenia*, a distinctive (and attractive) laminar stromatolite from the mid-Proterozoic of the Ozark Uplift of Missouri. (Value range G for individual slab)

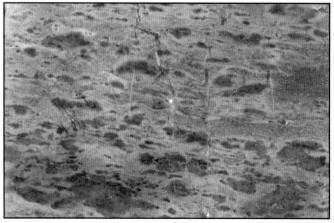

Fig. 07-42. Slab of epidote replaced small stromatolites, similar to previous photo.

The Mesoproterozoic saw the beginnings of a modern anoxic (oxygen containing) atmosphere and the continued formation of related beds of iron formation. However, unlike earlier times, beds of this biogenically produced iron-rich sediment are more localized. They, like the stromatolite *Ozarkcollenia*, appeared to have formed in shallow, volcanically formed lakes.

Fig. 07-45. Slab of iron formation different from the more ash laden types shown in the two previous photos. The pattern in this relatively volcanic ash free layer suggests vague stromatolitic patterns. Probably these patterns were formed by mats of moneran filaments growing on the bottom of shallow, volcanically formed lakes where the oxygen of photosynthesis precipitated iron oxide dissolved in the iron rich waters of the lake. Iron County, Missouri. (Value range G)

Fig. 07-43. Thin beds of iron formation interbedded with volcanic ash (tuff), which probably formed in lakes associated with nearby extensive volcanic activity. Oxygen produced by cyanobacteria either in the water or growing on the lake bottom reacted with dissolved iron salts and precipitated the iron as these beds of hematite mixed with volcanic ash from Iron County, Missouri. These are some of the younger iron formation beds in the Precambrian, harking back to the precipitation of iron in thick beds formed a few tens of million years earlier in other parts of the world. Iron County, Missouri, is named for the various types of iron deposits of mid-Proterozoic age that occur there. (Value range G)

Fig. 07-46. Close-up of slab of iron formation from same area as previous photo.

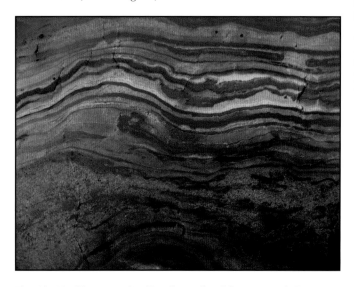

Fig. 07-44. Close-up of a slice through mid-Proterozoic iron formation, Iron County, Missouri. (Value range G)

Found in beds of volcanic ash (now converted to a rock called tuff) in Mesoproterozoic rocks are distinctive patterns believed to have been produced by mats of monerans growing on the bottom of shallow, volcanically formed lakes. Known as mottled-moneran-mats (mmm), they occur worldwide in similar settings as that of the Missouri Ozarks.

Fig. 07-47. This distinctive pattern is (probably) a consequence of some type of moneran mat growing on the surface of volcanic ash layers in very shallow water. A mat of blue-green algae (cyanobacteria) would become established, then a fall of ash would cover it. It would again re-establish itself and the process would be repeated again and again. This alternating sequence of moneran mat and ash fall produced this distinctive pattern in volcanic ash beds of the mid-Proterozoic of the Ozarks. Almost identical occurrences like this are found in rocks of the same age in northern Australia. Such patterns are sometimes referred to as mottled-moneran-mats (mmm). Cope Hollow Formation, Reynolds County, Missouri.

Fig. 07-48. Pattern produced in volcanic ash beds (tuffs) from alternating moneran mats and thin beds of volcanic ash. The moneran mat (probably cyanobacteria growing in a shallow body of water) would be covered by volcanic ash. The mat would re-establish itself repeatedly, forming this pattern. On this slab is superimposed a pattern formed at a later time known as Lesagang Rings, which is something different from the mottled-moneran-mat structure (mmm). Mid-Proterozoic tuffs, Northern Australia. Almost identical structures are found in volcanic tuffs of the same age in the Ozarks of Missouri. These Australian mottled-moneran-mats have been placed on the rockhound and fossil market. (Value range F)

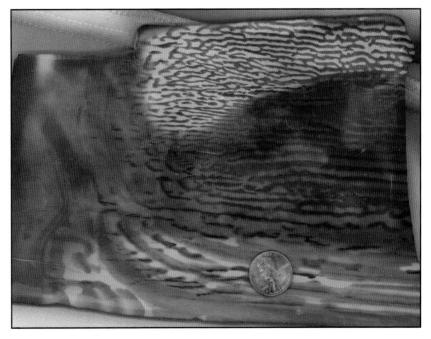

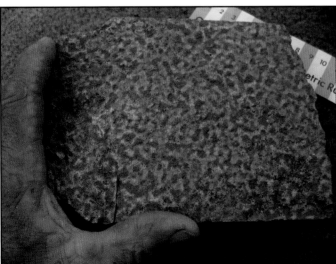

Fig. 07-49. Mottled-moneran-mat (mmm) slab from volcanic ash beds of western Reynolds County, Missouri. (Value range G)

Fig. 07-51. Mottled-moneran-mat slab in purple volcanic ash, Madison County, Missouri. These distinctive patterns are found associated with bedded volcanic ash beds (tuffs) at a number of localities in 1.5 billion year old volcanic sequences of the Missouri Ozarks.

Fig. 07-50. Iron rich, purple volcanic tuff has this pronounced mmm (mottled-moneran-mat) structure. Presumed organic material from a moneran mat allowed iron oxide to be removed from near the organic material, producing this distinctive pattern. Like a stromatolite, these probably represent phenomena produced by the chemical effects of a community of micro-organisms.

Possibly related to the formation of mottled-moneran-mats and of about the same age are a number of puzzling structures first brought to the attention of geologists by C. D. Walcott. These occur, like the stromatolites, in strata of the Belt Supergroup of the western states and provinces of North America.

Fig. 07-52. Outcrops of black Newland Limestone of the Belt Supergroup, west of White Sulphur Springs, Montana. A variety of puzzling algae structures occur in these rocks in association with low domal stromatolites. One of C. D. Walcott's localities.

Fig. 07-53. Outcrop of black Newland Limestone of the Belt Supergroup, west of White Sulphur Springs, Montana. These limestones contain a number of different types of stromatolites and other puzzling structures considered by C. D. Walcott to be peculiar stromatolites.

Fig. 07-54. *Newlandia* sp. Distinctive structures originally described by Walcott from the Belt Mts., Montana. Such structures were considered by him as types of algal colonies viz. types of stromatolites. A variety of such structures occur in the Mesoproterozoic Belt Supergroup of Montana, but there is still ambivalence as to the origin of many of them. Some may be concretions, others are probably aberrant stromatolites. The "Treatise on Invertebrate Paleontology," Part W, has most of them classified as pseudofossils. Unlike most pseudofossils, these occur in reef-like masses suggesting biogenicity, a fact noted by C. D. Walcott. (Value range F)

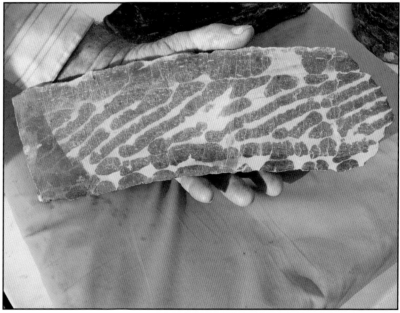

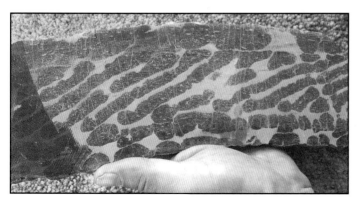

Fig. 07-55. *Newlandia frondosa* Walcott, 1914. A distinctive and peculiar structure found in the Mesoproterozoic Belt Supergroup of western Montana. Walcott considered *Newlandia* as a type of algae. It has been variously placed as a pseudofossil and as a dubiofossil. Its occurrence in outcrops of the Belt Mountains of Montana suggests reef-like structures that can be seen on canyon walls and is considered by this author to be a type of aberrant stromatolite. This is a slab sliced from a *Newlandia* "colony." (Value range F)

Fig. 07-56. Slab of the large type of *Newlandia* (*Newlandia frondosa*). Newland limestone, Belt Super Group, Townsend, Montana. (Value range F)

Fig. 07-57. Group of three slabs of *Newlandia frondosa*, Walcott 1914. This distinctive stromatolite from the Newland Limestone near Townsend Montana is found in the Precambrian of North America as well as in Australia.. (Value range G)

Fig. 07-58. Australian *Newlandia* sp. This distinctive structure found in Northwestern Australia is quite similar to *Newlandia* from Montana. A number of puzzling structures occur in the Precambrian of Australia that also occur in North America, such as these specimens. This structure is known in the rockhound world as Zebra Rock. It has a different color from the Montana *Newlandia* but this is easily explained as a consequence of weathering (lateriteization) under the arid conditions of Australia. Ranford Formation, Kununurra, northwestern Australia. (Value range F)

Fig. 07-59. Group of Zebra Rock (*Newlandia*) slabs. Kununurra, East Kimberley Range of Western Australia. Ranford Formation. (Value range G for each slab)

Fig. 07-60. *Newlandia lamellose* Walcott 1914. Small variety of *Newlandia*, which, like other forms of *Newlandia*, form reef-like structures in the Newland Limestone. Near Townsend Montana. (Value range G)

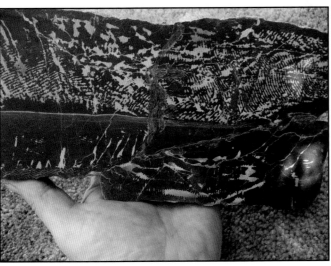

Fig. 07-61. *Newlandia lamellose* Walcott 1914. A somewhat jumbled mass of this peculiar stromatolite. Newland Limestone, Townsend, Montana. (Value range F)

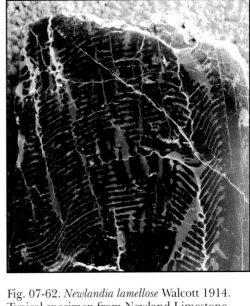

Fig. 07-62. *Newlandia lamellose* Walcott 1914. Typical specimen from Newland Limestone, Townsend Montana.

Fig. 07-63. *Copperia* sp. Walcott 1914. Another puzzling stromatolite from the Newland Limestone, White Sulphur Springs, Montana.

Occurring also in Belt strata are horizons containing small concave disks considered at one time to be inarticulate (primitive) brachiopods. These are fossils, but like so many other Precambrian fossils, they are of algal origin and may be similar to *Carelozoon* and *Corycium*, both known from the Grenville Series and also from the Precambrian of Finland.

Fig. 07-64. *Chuaria* sp. A small broad cap-like fossil, once considered to be a type of primitive brachiopod but now considered as a type of very large Protista called an acritarch. *Chuaria* can locally occur in abundance on the bedding planes of shale beds of the Belt Supergroup. The original description of this fossil was by C. D. Walcott from Belt age strata in the lower part of the Grand Canyon. Greyson Shale, Belt Supergroup, Townsend Montana. (Value range H)

Fig. 07-65. Slab of Greyson Shale with numerous *Chuaria* sp. Townsend, Montana.

Also of algal origin are the fossils mistaken by Charles Walcott for eurypterid fragments in Belt sediments. These are similar to, and probably fragments of, moranids (Figs. 06-07 and 06-08).

Fig. 07-66. Moranid fragment that resembles half of a eurypterid body segment (turgite). Greyson shale, Townsend, Montana. C. D. Walcott considered such fossils as fragments of eurypterids and felt that the reason few animal fossils were found in most Precambrian strata was because these sediments were deposited in large lakes consisting of fresh rather than salt water, which supports normal marine animals.

Medusiform fossils, dubiofossils, and pseudofossils. Starting with the Paleoproterozoic are found various medusiform-like objects that occur on bedding planes of strata. Originally interpreted as impressions of medusa or jellyfish, they remain puzzling and ubiquitous. Many of these objects appear biogenic, others are interpreted as gas evasion structures. Determination of their biogenic origin is significant as it might throw light on the time of appearance of the earth's first true animals, usually considered by biologists to have been some sort of Cnidarian—the phylum to which jellyfish belong.

Fig. 07-67. Medusoid dubiofossils from near the top of the Belt Supergroup of northwestern Montana. Creases near the rim of these dubiofossils suggests a fossil medusa. If these were found in younger strata they would be considered as medusoid fossils. These occur on bedding planes of strata below the presumed glacial deposits of "Snowball Earth," hence are more suspect as being true jellyfish (and hence multicelled animals).

Fig. 07-69. Medusiform trace fossils. These traces of a worm-like animal reaching out and feeding from its burrow can resemble fossil jellyfish and these have been confused with jellyfish impressions in the literature of paleontology. Phanerozoic, western Colorado. (Value range F)

Fig. 07-68. Undoubted? medusa impressions. Such jellyfish impressions have been found in large numbers on bedding planes of sandstones of various age; these are Cambrian. Many of these fossil jellyfish have been widely distributed. Mt. Simon Sandstone, Middle Cambrian, Mosinee Wisconsin. (Value range F)

Bibliography

Dawson, J. W. "On the structure of certain organic remains in the Laurentian Limestones of Canada." *Quarterly Journal of the Geological Society of London*, Vol. 21, 1865, pp 51-59.

Fedonkin, Mikhail A., and Ellis L Yochelson. Middle Proterozoic (1.5 Ga) "*Horodyskia moniliformis* Yochelson and Fedonkin, the Oldest Known Tissue-Grade Colonial Eucaryote." Smithsonian Institution Press, 2002.

Gould, Stephen J. "Bathybius and Eozoon," in *The Panda's Thumb*. W. W. Norton Co., New York and London. 1980.

Hofmann, Hans J. "Precambrian fossils, pseudofossils and Problematica in Canada." *Geological Survey of Canada*, Bulletin 189, 1971.

Hofmann, Hans J., Guy M. Narbonne, and J. D. Aitken. "Ediacaran remains from intertillite beds in northwestern Canada." *Geology*, Vol. 18, 1990, p. 1199-1202.

Rezak, Richard. "Stromatolites of the Belt Series in Glacier National Park and Vicinity, Montana." U S Geological Professional Paper 294-D., 1957, pp. 127-165.

Schopf, J. W. "Tempo and Mode of Proterozoic Evolution." In J. W. Schopf and C. Klein, eds., *The Proterozoic Biosphere: A Multidisciplinary Study*. Cambridge: Cambridge University Press, 1992.

Stinchcomb, Bruce L. "Possible biogenic structures in Prebatholithic tuffs of the Missouri Precambrian." *Transactions of Missouri Academy of Sciences* (abstract), 2006.

Walcott, Charles D. "Pre-Cambrian Algonkian algal flora." Smithsonian Institution Miscellaneous Collections, Vol. 64. No. 2, 1914, pp. 77-156.

Chapter Eight

The Neoproterozoic and Evolutionary Experimentation

The Neoproterozoic is the last major subdivision of the Precambrian. Its time span ranges from some 800 million years to some 540 million years ago, encompassing a time when major advancements of life took place. Somewhere around 540 million years ago, that vast span of geologic time called the Precambrian ended and the Cambrian Period, with its diversity of animal life, began. Early Neoproterozoic time saw an earth similar to that of the Mesoproterozoic, and that was not too different from the Paleoproterozoic. Through all of this long time span, cyanobacteria appear to be the dominant forms of life. Stromatolites predominate, notwithstanding the periodic paleontologic puzzles that occur here and there, as they are predominantly the products of cyanobacterial life processes. A seascape dominated primarily by stromatolites was the norm in the early Neoproterozoic as well, but was followed by an event or series of events, still little understood, that would result in complex life appearing at the end of the Precambrian.

As in the Mesoproterozoic, there are occasional problematic "fossils," the interpretation of which varies with the interpreter.

Fig. 08-01. *Archaeozoon acadiense* Matthew 1890. A slice through one of the "zoons," originally suggested to have been some sort of giant protozoan or protista but now recognized as a type of stromatolite. Green Head Group, Green Head near Saint John, New Brunswick, Canada. (Value range F)

Fig. 08-02. *Archaeozoon acadiense* Matthew 1890. A sliced, single specimen of this distinctive fossil, one of the first stromatolites to be identified. Its identity as a stromatolite didn't come until twenty-four years after it was described in the geologic literature. Green Head Group, Green Head, St. John, New Brunswick, Canada (Value range F)

Fig. 08-03. A stromatolite preserved in dolomite from a sequence of flat lying, late Proterozoic strata outcropping (Sibley Series) north of Lake Superior and probably associated with the Lake Superior rift system. Stromatolites like this, vague and without a distinctive pattern, are not usually highly collectible. This specimen is preserved in dolomite and the process of converting the original limestone into dolomite makes the stromatolite structure vague. (Value range for similar material H)

Fig. 08-05. Cubes and other geometric shapes are worked by artisans from these distinctive stromatolites that come from Bolivia and are currently widely distributed through the rock hound market. Some labels state them as being from Peru, however this is where they are polished; the outcrops from which they come are in Bolivia. They are suggestive of stromatolite morphologies or types of the mid or late Proterozoic. (Value range G for single specimen)

Fig. 08-04. Attractive late Proterozoic stromatolites from Bolivia have been widely distributed in the fossil market through the Tucson, Arizona show. These stromatolites, like many other occurrences, are distinctive in both color and morphology. They are sometimes cut into blocks or other polygons, which produce interesting patterns. Their age is variously given as mid-Proterozoic or early Neoproterozoic. (Value range F)

Fig. 08-06. A single cube cut from Bolivian stromatolites. This form is suggestive of stromatolites of the form genus *Greysonia* sp. and characteristic of the late Precambrian. (Value range G)

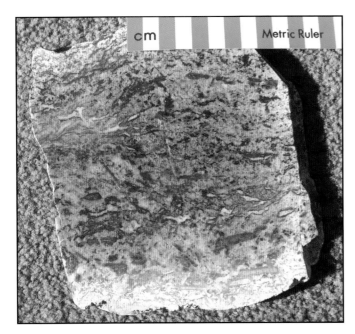

Fig. 08-07. Packstone. Granular sediment containing numerous fragments of stromatolites compose this distinctive sedimentary rock known as packstone. The packstone represented by this slab occurs between "fingers" of the digitate stromatolite from genus *Baicalia* sp. Packstone of the late Precambrian as well as of the early Paleozoic can include small shell-like fossils, and phosphate rich packstones of late Precambrian age in China have yielded groups of phosphate-replaced cells representing microscopic fossil eukaryotes. Julius River, Trowutta, Tasmania, Australia. (Value range F)

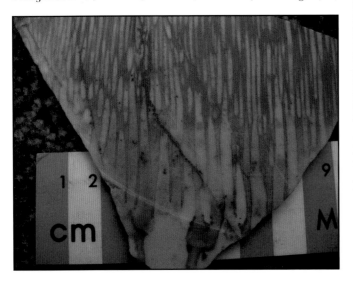

Fig. 08-08. *Tigillites bohmei* Branaugh. A Precambrian enigma, these "trace fossils" have been described as vertical burrows similar to *Scolithus* (Figs. 08-32 to 08-35), but they are from the Proterozoic of Arizona. They also have a "signature" more suggestive of a strange type of stromatolite than that of a trace fossil. These are "puzzling" fossils. (Value range F or E, horizon is supposedly "worked out")

The middle part of the Neoproterozoic presents some worldwide puzzles, one of which involves the sediments considered to be glacial deposits on a scale so vast that the time period some 700 million years ago has been called the era of "Snowball Earth." This era represented one of the coldest periods in earth's history, when parts of the planet's oceans froze—accompanied by a major drop in sea level and the buildup of ice that formed vast regions of glaciers. Such a deep freeze put considerable stress on the biosphere, where adversity seems to have encouraged an accelerated rate of evolution. One of the consequences resulting from Snowball Earth was various evolutionary "experiments," made up of eukaryotic celled life forms, and the appearance of the earth's first undoubted animals.

Fig. 08-09. *Tigillites bohmei*, Branaugh. Top, same specimen as in previous photo; note expansion of "burrows" toward the top of the slab. This is atypical of worm burrows and suggests that this puzzling structure may be a type of pseudofossil or a dubiofossil—vertical "worm" burrows do not normally do this! Bottom, horizontal slice across burrows. Mescal Limestone, Apache Group, Giacoma's Camp, Arizona. (Value range F)

Among these "experiments" were the vendozoans or ediacaran organisms of the late Precambrian. First recognized in Southeastern Australia in the Ediacaran Hills of the Flinders Range, these peculiar bilaterally and radially symmetrical fossils (vendozoans) have been interpreted in a number of novel ways.

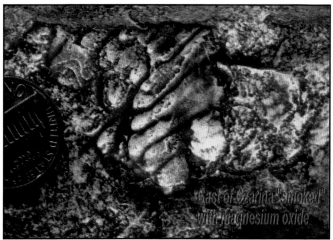

Fig. 08-11. Cast of *Czarina* that has been coated with magnesium oxide. This is a dubiofossil, suggestive of the clear and sometimes distinctive impressions of vendozoans. (Value range H, as a cast)

Fig. 08-10. The time of appearance of the first life on land as determined from the fossil record is muddy and unclear. Candidates for the earliest land life are photosynthetic life forms, as other, "heterotrophic" organisms would have had to rely upon photosynthetic organisms as food; hence, photosynthetic life had to come first. Some candidates for the earth's first land life are lichens (a symbiosis between cyanobacteria and fungi), mosses, and liverworts. Lichens are not plants; the other two are primitive, non-vascular plants that rely upon wet or damp surfaces to grow. This dubiofossil is an example of what are sometimes found as candidates for the first land life; it is often difficult to determine if such "fossils" are biogenic or not. These examples are found in black sandstone cobbles (possibly Neoproterozoic in age) of an Ozark river and were interpreted as impressions of liverworts or lichens. They have also been interpreted as possible Ediacarian organisms from the seemingly clear impression in the matrix. Edicarian organisms, or vendozoans, are themselves interpreted by some as lichens, and the late Proterozoic as being an age of lichens. Lichens are leathery, and potentially would leave a clear impression like this in sediments as a consequence of this texture. Named *Czarina* after Czar Knob near where it was found, this is also possibly a pseudofossil, that is, it is a dubiofossil. (Value range F)

Fig. 08-12. Elongate and isolated forms of *Czarina*. Morphological variation characterizes these dubiofossils; such variation, however, is also a characteristic of lichens. Black sandstone boulders found along the west fork of the Black River in the Missouri Ozarks yield these dubiofossils. Originally thought to be derived from a mostly buried sequence of very late Proterozoic strata (Ediacarian), they were considered as possible vendozoans. Another suggestion is that they are fossil lichens. Vendozoans have been considered as possible marine lichens, and the late Neoproterozoic after "Snowball Earth" to have been an age of lichens. Lichens represent a symbiotic relationship between photosynthetic algae and a fungi and are **not** plants. (Value range E)

The most conservative interpretation is that vendozoans are representative of early invertebrates, soft bodied ancestors of Cnidarians such as jellyfish and sea pens.

Another interpretation is that vendozoans represent an entirely extinct life form, an unsuccessful evolutionary experiment at the kingdom level. Vendozoan fossils, unlike those of undoubted animals that lack hard parts, suggest organisms that had a tough, leathery texture capable of leaving distinct impressions in sediments such as sand or silt—sediment that is usually not associated with good fossil preservation of soft bodied animals.

Fig. 08-13. Dipping or tilted bedding plane containing numerous impressions of vendozoans. In the late Precambrian occur a variety of puzzling, circular and bilaterally symmetrical fossils of disputed taxonomic position collectively referred to as vendozoans, after the Russian Vendian or latest Precambrian. Vendozoans have been considered as ancestors of Cambrian animals and modern invertebrates. In this photo, the large form below the hammer would be a large pennatulate cnidarian, spindle-shaped forms to the left would be considered sea pens, and radially symmetrical forms would be medusoids or jellyfish. This conservative interpretation has been challenged, in part, because soft bodied animals like jellyfish and sea pens do not leave the distinct impressions like those shown here. Soft, fleshy animals leave only a faint, carbon film impression with little or no three-dimensionality. Advocates for a more exotic interpretation point out that to leave such distinct impressions as these, the organisms responsible for them would have had to be leathery and tough. They suggest that vendozoans might have been a type of lichen (which are leathery and tough) or may have been representatives of an extinct, experimental life form, possibly at the kingdom level. Mistaken Point fossil preserve, Cape Race, Newfoundland.

Fig. 08-14. Medusiform vendozoan to the right of spindle-shaped form. Outcrop at Mistaken Point fossil preserve, Cape Race, Newfoundland.

Fig. 08-15. Another scatter of vendozoan impressions on a bedding plane at Mistaken Point fossil preserve, eastern Newfoundland. Note the elongate spindle-shaped form just above a very elongate form in line from a projection of the hammer point. This spindle shaped form has a rim around it, a morphology not seen on other vendozoans. Note also the radially symmetrical medusiform vendozoan at bottom center.

Fig. 08-16. Bedding plane of dipping strata covered with numerous impressions of a variety of vendozoans. This concentration of vendozoans shows what a rich and phenomenal site the Mistaken Point exposures are. The site is now a paleontological preserve and has one of the most concentrated known occurrences of these peculiar fossils in the world. Many vendozoan occurrences exhibit only a few specimens, one here, one there—nothing like this concentration.

Fig. 08-17. Medusiform (circular or radially symmetrical vendozoan) to the left of the pick and spindle-shaped form below that. Mistaken Point paleontological preserve, eastern Newfoundland.

Fig. 08-19. Specimen of a portion of spindle-shaped vendozoan, collected in the 1960s, before the Mistaken Point site became a protected paleontological site. Note the depth of the impressions made by the organism; soft bodied animal impressions are never this distinct.

Fig. 08-18. Two spindle-shaped ("sea pen like") vendozoans parallel to each other to the left of the hammer. At the bottom left is a branching form; note also the small spindle just above the hammer's end. The Mistaken Point Formation (a metamorphosed mudstone) exhibits a number of cracks (joints) in the tilted sea cliff outcrop. Mistaken Point, Cape Race, Newfoundland.

Fig. 08-20. Impression of part of a spindle-shaped vendozoan from a Neoproterozoic sequence in the Carolina Slate Belt, similar to those from Mistaken Point Newfoundland. The lithology of these meta-morphosed mudstones is almost identical to that of Newfoundland. Rock Hole Creek, Stanly County, North Carolina. (Value range F)

Fig. 08-22. Weathered and abraded portion of large spindle-shaped vendozoan from Rock Hole Creek, Stanly County, North Carolina. Some of the vendozoans of both Newfoundland and North Carolina can be quite large.

Fig. 08-23. Possible attachment area of spindle-shaped ven-dozoan (middle of the slab). Spindle-shaped vendozoans are considered by some to have been attached to the ocean floor, and small, circular forms like these represent the attachment areas. Other vendozoan workers believe that the organisms lay on the sea floor and were an integral part of a moneran mat. Rock Hole Creek, Stanly County, North Carolina. (Value range G for comparable material)

Fig. 08-21. Bush-like form of vendozoan from meta-mudstones of North Carolina. Similar to this are some of the fossils in the vendo-zoan concentration of Fig. 08-16. The known vendozoan localities of North and South Carolina have limited numbers of specimens compared to the Cape Race locality in Newfoundland, but some of the organisms are the same or similar. Similar vendozoans are also known from England (Charnwood Forest), where they occur in similar hard, greenish, metamorphosed mudstone. Vendozoans like these might also occur in Morocco, where strata of this type and age occur. From Rock Hole Creek, Stanly County, North Caro-lina. (Value range E for comparable material)

The third interpretation is that vendozoans are marine lichens. Lichens represent a symbiosis between fungi and cyanobacteria—a collaboration between two cell types, one fungal, the other moneran. They have a tough and leathery texture and some paleontologists have suggested that the last half of the Neoproterozoic was an age of lichens. In many cases, vendozoans seem to be associated with moneran mats and may have lain on the sea floor, intimately incorporated into parts of this mat. At the very end of the Neoproterozoic are found strata carrying tracks and trails (trace fossils), and small cone and cylinder shaped fossils such as *Wyattia* and *Cloudina*.

Fig. 08-25. *Nemiana* sp., also known as *Beltanelliformis* and considered by some Russian workers as a type of green algae. Circular medusoid fossils of the Neoproterozoic are difficult to interpret. *Nemiana* sp. is one vendozoan that has come upon the fossil market. Like other vendozoans, it appears to have had a tough leathery texture that left distinct impressions in sediments and makes, if well preserved, nice clear fossils. (Value range F)

Fig. 08-24. *Nemiana simplex*. These circular vendozoans occur on bedding planes of greenish sandstone layers that crop out along the White Sea region of Russia. Bedding planes can be covered with such vendozoans, closely packed together. Like other, well preserved Ediacarian fossils, these suggest a tough, leathery organism such as a lichen. As a result, it has been suggested that vendozoans were a type of marine lichen and that the appearance of animals in the Cambrian Period was preceded by an earlier age of lichens. Vendozoans have also been suggested as representing a completely extinct life form at the kingdom level, and may have been an example of an "unsuccessful evolutionary experiment" that preceded the "experiment" resulting in the animal and plant life of the Cambrian radiation event. These are one of the few vendozoan fossils to come in quantity upon the fossil market. (Value range E)

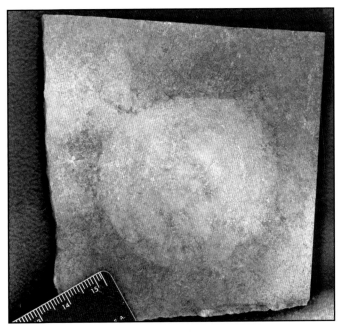

Fig. 08-26. Medusiform vendozoan from quartzites of the Ediacarian Hills, Flinders Range, eastern Australia. These were the first Ediacarian fossils described from quartzite or hard sandstone layers (Pound Quartzite) of the very late Precambrian of Australia. (Value range D)

Fig. 08-27. Vague impression of a medusiform vendozoan from Ediacarian Hills, Flinders Range, Australia. A few superb specimens of these interesting and scientifically valuable fossils came onto the fossil market a few years ago, however the entire range has since been made a paleontological preserve and all collecting is strictly prohibited. The Pound Quartzite and the Ediacarian biota (biota rather than fauna, as they may not be animals) extends over a considerable area. A protected paleontological preserve makes sense for a limited occurrence such as the Mistaken Point locality in Newfoundland, but this Australian material extends over a considerable area. It is the author's opinion that paleontology is best served through material being collected and brought into the hands of interested persons, either through individual collecting or through the fossil market rather than being "locked up" by paleontological "preservationists."

Fig. 08-28. "*Eldonia*" sp. This radially symmetrical, medusiform fossil is from the Phanerozoic (Lowermost Ordovician), hence it is not a true vendozoan as these are generally restricted to strata of the Late Precambrian. This fossil, in hard sandstone similar to that of the Australian Flinders Range material, is however a clear impression of a soft bodied "leathery" organism. The genus *Eldonia* is known from the Cambrian Burgess shale, at which locality it is preserved as a thin film of graphite and clay minerals and is undoubtedly an animal, possibly an early holothurian (sea cucumber). These fossils, which appeared upon the fossil market, are impressions of a much firmer and leathery-like organism, which, if Precambrian, would be considered a vendozoan. Lower Ordovician, Mesissi, Morocco. (Value range D)

Near the beginning of the Paleozoic, trace fossils become more varied and abundant in rock sequences that seem to span the Precambrian-Cambrian boundary. Above this, now in strata of the Paleozoic Era, a variety of puzzling small fossils occur at the very beginning of the Cambrian Period. This occurrence is known as the Tommotian; it is the pre-trilobite portion of the Cambrian Period, that "age of trilobites." The Tommotian is followed by the Olenellus zone, named after the trilobite genus *Olenellus*, one of the earliest trilobites to appear in the fossil record.

Fig. 08-29. *Wyattia* sp. Small, cone shaped fossils, difficult to see individually and to photograph, occur on weathered surfaces of a Late Precambrian dolomite bed in the Inyo Mountains of Southern California. In somewhat younger rocks, generally considered as lowermost Cambrian, similar but better preserved small cone shaped fossils occur. These are the "small shellies" of the Tommotian, the early-most part of the Cambrian. Other small, shelled life forms such as *Cloudia* also occur just before the Cambrian.

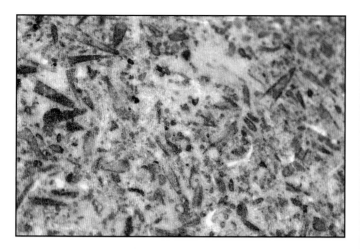

Fig. 08-30. *Wyattia* like fossils from low in the Cambrian of Missouri. These small fossils, consisting of cone shaped shells, first appear at the very end of the Neoproterozoic. (Value range G)

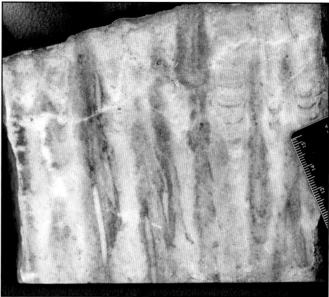

Fig. 08-32. *Scolithus linearus* Haldeman 1840. Longitudinal section of these distinctive trace fossils. *Scolithus* is known from the very beginning of the Phanerozoic fossil record and occurs in what some geologists consider as latest Precambrian strata. *Scolithus* occurs earlier than trilobites. The specimens shown here occur in a sequence of strata—of which the bottom is considered to be latest Proterozoic in age, *Scolithus* occurs midway in the sequence, and trilobites occur at the top of the sequence. *Scolithus* is a trace fossil believed to have been made by a phoronid worm, one of the many "worm phyla." Look-alikes occur in much more ancient strata than this latest Proterozoic or earlymost Paleozoic quartzite from eastern Tennessee. Chilthowee Formation, Montvale Springs, Tennessee. (Value range G)

Fig. 08-31. *Scolithus linearis* Haldeman 1840 (also as *Skolithos*). The openings of vertical burrows perpendicular to the bedding plane of a sandstone slab: burrow entrances in this specimen show "collars" surrounding each burrow. *Scolithus* is a common trace fossil that predates other, better known Cambrian life forms such as trilobites. *Scolithus*-like dubiofossils occur in earlier strata, such as *Tigillites* (Figs. 08-09, 06-16, and 06-17), but the identification of these as being true trace fossils is questioned. (Value range G)

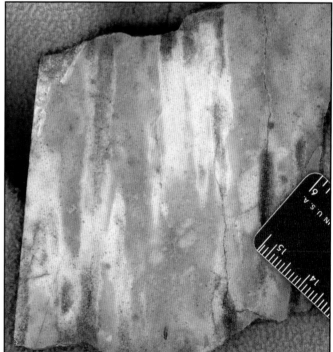

Fig. 08-33. *Scolithus linearis.* Specimen from a glacial erratic, possibly Lower Cambrian in age but possibly even latest Precambrian, as *Scolithus* appears at the very end of the Neoproterozoic. (Value range G)

Fig. 08-34. Mesoproterozoic strata world wide have yielded metazoan-like trace fossils, but like most Precambrian non-stromatolite fossils, these are of infrequent occurrence. One of these consists of a string or a linear arrangement of circular bumps or compressions decreasing in size towards both ends of the "string." Another is a vertical burrow-like form resembling the vertical burrow *Scolithus*. *Scolithus*–like dubiofossils and pseudofossils can be made by small, vertically rising plumes of water through sediments, so called fluid-evasion structures. Similar *Scolithus*-like structures can also be formed in fluid lava from gas bubbles rising through the molten rock. Distinguishing burrows or tracks made by animals from similar looking structures made by non-biogenic means can be quite vexing. These are the tops of *Scolithus* burrows on a sandstone (quartzite) bedding plane. (Value range G)

Fig. 08-36. Distinct, single burrow filling of *Scolithus*. Chilthowee Quartzite, Montvale Springs, Eastern Tennessee. (Value range G)

Fig. 08-37. Quartzite block with horizontal and vertical sections of *Scolithus*. Chilthowee Quartzite, Montvale Springs, Tennessee. (Value range F)

Fig. 08-35. Slab of Chilthowee Quartzite with entrance depressions of the vertical burrows of *Scolithus*. These have been highlighted with iron oxide. Chilthowee Quartzite, Chilthowee Mountain, Montvale, Tennessee. (Value range G)

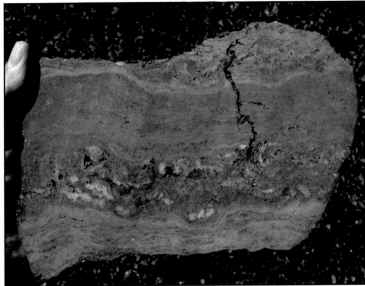

Fig. 08-40. Possible laminar stromatolites from what are possibly late Precambrian ocherous chert beds southwest of Fredericktown, Missouri. (Value range G)

Fig. 08-38. Foolers! These vertical "burrows" in **basalt** resemble *Scolithus* sp. The basalt layer in which they occur looks like dirty sandstone and is interbedded with sedimentary rocks containing stromatolites. Being present in basalt, an igneous rock, they obviously were not made by worms but rather were made by bubbles of gas, rising upward through what was molten rock. Belt Supergroup, West Glacier, Montana.

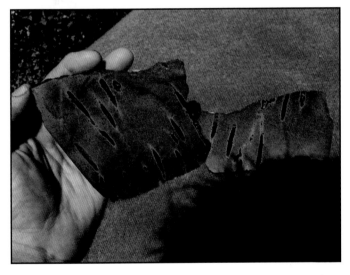

Fig. 08-39. Slabs of "*Scolithus*"- like "burrows" that originated from rising gas bubbles in molten rock. Belt Series, West Glacier, Montana. (Value range H)

Fig. 08-41. Oncolites from late Neoproterozoic limestone of the Inyo Mountains, Southern California. A number of nice oncolite slabs from the Inyo and Marble Mountains of Southern California have shown up on the fossil market; they are from undoubted Cambrian strata and are associated with trilobite fragments. The oncolites shown here are from a horizon well below that containing Cambrian fossils, hence certainly late Proterozoic. (Value range H)

Fig. 08-42. *Salterella* sp. Similar to some small calcareous fossils found in the latest Proterozoic, but larger, these small bullet-shaped fossils are associated with some of the earliest trilobites. *Salterella* has been placed in its own phylum, Phylum Agmata, as it has no characteristics common with any modern phyla. When it occurs, *Salterella* can occur in abundance. Internal molds to the left, black limestone containing *Salterella* (circles) to the right. (Value range H)

Fig. 08-43. *Salterella* sp. These are internal molds of the bullet-like tests of this earlymost Cambrian fossil, Corner Brook, Newfoundland.

Bibliography

Cloud, Preston. "The Biosphere." *Scientific American*, Volume 249, 1983, pg. 176-187.

Glaessner, M. F. *The Dawn of Animal Life: A Biohistorical Study.* Cambridge, London: Cambridge University Press, 1984.

Gould, Stephen J. *Death and Transfiguration in the Flamingo's Smile.* New York and London: W. W. Norton Co., 1983.

Brasier, Martin, and Jonathan Antcliffe. "Decoding the Ediacaran Enigma." *Science*, Vol. 305, No. 5687, 2004, pp. 1115-1117.

McMenamin, Mark A. S., and Dianna L. Schulte McMenamin. *The Emergence of Animals: The Cambrian Breakthrough.* New York: Columbia University Press, 1989.

Narbonne, Guy N. "Modular Construction of Early Ediacarian Complex Life Forms." *Science*, Vol. 305, 2004, pp. 1141-1144.

Teichert, Curt. "Treatise on Invertebrate Paleontology." Part W. *Miscellanea, Supplement 1, Trace Fossils and Problematica, 2nd Edition.* The Geological Society of America and University of Kansas, 1975.

Wright, Karen. "When Life was Odd." *Discover Magazine*, Vol. 18, Number 3, 1997.

Chapter Nine

Cambrian Trilobites

Lower Cambrian Trilobites

As one goes upward through strata of the latest Precambrian, all of a sudden small fossil shells occur, accompanied by abundant fossil burrows and trails; you have just crossed into strata representative of the Cambrian period with its diverse animal life. This sudden diversification of life in the fossil record is known as the Cambrian radiation event. This is the point at which most popular and non-technical books on fossils begin. It's also at this part of earth history that many fossil-philes make the remark that "everything older than the Cambrian is just so much algae!"

Above strata yielding the small, peculiar shell-like fossils, one might find the fossils of these trilobites. Trilobites are arthropods that were dominant players in the earth's first flowering of life. The first trilobites are known as olenellids. Olenellids were primitive trilobites with a large number of segments and a distinctive head or cephalon. Specimens in Figs. 09-01 to 09-18 are olenellids; all are trilobites from the earliest part of the Cambrian Period, the Lower Cambrian.

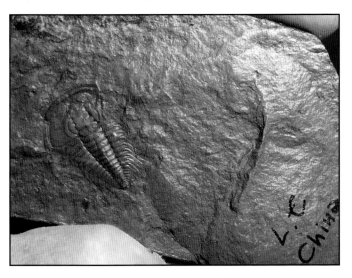

Fig. 09-001. *Redlichia* sp. An olenellid trilobite found in China and other parts of Asia. Lower Cambrian, Hubbei Province, China. The olenellid trilobites are the earliest trilobites to appear in the fossil record, occurring in the Lower Cambrian.

Fig. 09-003. *Olenellus clarki* (Resser) Marble Mts., California. Trilobite. Moss-like structures at the right are dendrites, that is, radiating crystals (fractuals) of manganese oxide. (Value range G)

Fig. 09-002. *Olenellus fremonti* Walcott. A trilobite, widely collected in the past from the Latham Shale of the Marble Mts., southern California. The locality for these is no longer available as it is now part of Death Valley National Park. (Value range G)

Fig. 09-004. *Paedumias* sp. A complete specimen of this olenellid trilobite from the Lower Cambrian Rome Formation, which outcrops within the environs of Montevallo, Alabama, part of the southernmost part of the Appalachians. (Value range C)

Below:
Fig. 09-005. Views of a superb specimen of *Olenellus thompsoni*, showing part and counterpart. Rome Formation, Montevallo, Alabama. Note highly segmented "tail" or pygidium, a characteristic of many Lower Cambrian trilobites and an evolutionary link to their highly segmented "worm like" ancestors of the Precambrian. (Value range C)

Fig. 09-006. Another view of *Olenellus thompsoni*, Rome Formation.

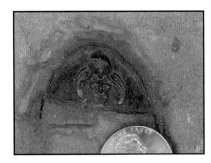

Fig. 09-007. Cephalon or "head" of *Olenellus* sp. The most common occurrence of this early trilobite is the cephalon. Trilobites would molt and fragmented specimens like this usually represent such molted exoskeletons. Complete specimens are much rarer and usually represent individual animals that perished in the sediments (now rock) in which they are found. (Value range H)

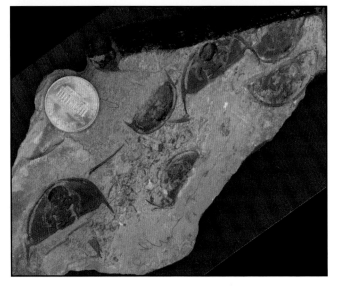

Fig. 09-008. Group of heads of *Olenellus* sp. Rome Formation, Montevallo, Alabama. (Value range G)

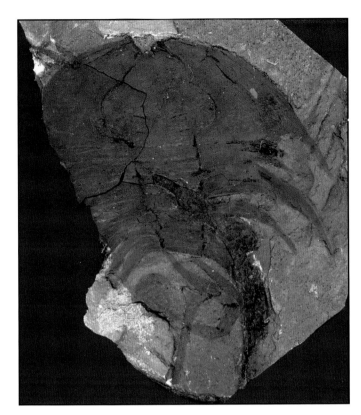

Fig. 09-011. Very spiny Olenellid trilobite, *Bristolia bristolensis* Resser, Marble Mts., southern California. Casts of this rare and distinctive trilobite have been widely distributed. (Value range H)

Fig. 09-009. Large, somewhat fragmented specimen of *Paedumias* from Lower Cambrian strata at the Getz Farm, Kinzers, near Lancaster, Pennsylvania. Unfortunately this locality has been swallowed up by urbanization from Lancaster. Some large and interesting arthropods besides trilobites, such as *Anomalocaris*, came from this locality in the nineteenth century. (Value range F)

Fig. 09-012. Impression of *Wanneria* sp. from Kinzers, Lancaster, Pennsylvania. The thorax has been damaged prior to burial in sediment. Fossils from this locality were some of the first from the earliest part of the Cambrian to be described. (Value range E)

Fig. 09-010. *Olenellus fremontia* (Walcott) Marble Mountains, California (cast). This cast of a complete specimen, raised in high relief by carving, has been widely distributed in the trilobite collecting community. (Value range F)

Fig. 09-013. Left: *Olenellus fremontia*; right: *Bristolia* sp. Early Cambrian trilobites are often distorted like this specimen from earth movements associated with mountain building. They are also often associated with slaty shale of a greenish or yellowish color. Nopah Range, Southern California.

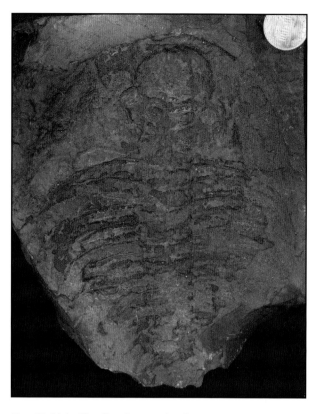

Fig. 09-014. *Olenellus thompsoni*. A large specimen, missing the pygidium, from the Getz Farm, Kinzers, near Lancaster, Pennsylvania. (Value range E)

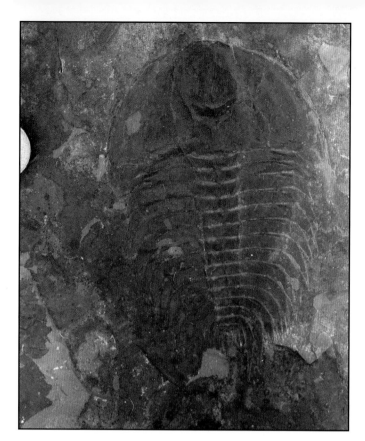

Fig. 09-017. *Wanneria walcottana*. A relatively large and complete impression of this olenellid trilobite. *Wanneria* has lobes extending from the pygidium and has a textured surface on the exoskeleton as well as being relatively large. Eager Formation, Fort Steele, British Columbia, Canada. (Value range D)

Fig. 09-015. *Paedeumias* sp. Part and counterpart in red, slaty shale. Eager Formation, Fort Steele, British Columbia, Canada. (Value range F)

Fig. 09-016. *Olenellus* sp. Small, iron stained specimen typical of occurrences of olenellid trilobites. Eager Formation, Fort Steele, British Columbia, Canada.

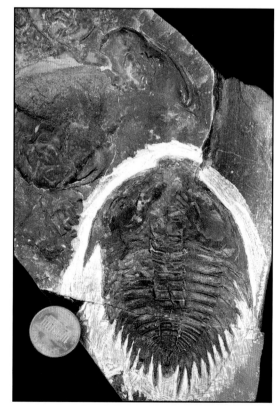

Fig. 09-018. *Wanneria* sp. and partial specimen. Eager Formation, Fort Steele, British Columbia, Canada. (Value range E)

Non-olenellid trilobites of probable Lower Cambrian age are shown next.

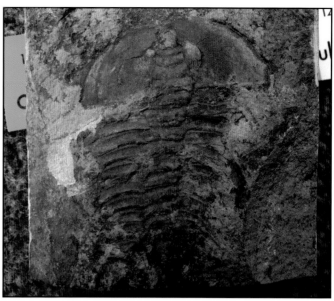

Fig. 09-019. *Nevadia weeksi.* Part and counterpart of this olenellid with a relatively small cephalon. Montezuma Range, Esmeralda County, Nevada (Value range F)

Fig. 09-020. *Nevadia weeksi.* Montezuma Range, Esmeralda County, Nevada.

These are trilobites that have come on the fossil market from Morocco. They are probably of late Lower Cambrian or early-most Middle Cambrian of the Atlantic or Avalonian Province.

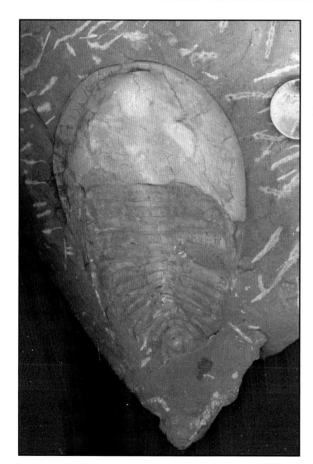

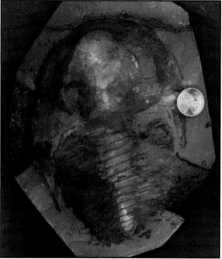

Fig. 09-022. *Cambropallas telesto (Andalusiana).* Typical specimen available on the fossil market, Lower Cambrian, Morocco. (Value range E)

Fig. 09-023. *Cambropallas telesto,* Dibel Ougrat, Morocco. Specimen prepared with chisel marks radiating from the fossil. These trilobites, quarried from a ferruginous (iron bearing) siltstone, are easily prepared and are prepared locally. Rumors have circulated that these are not actual specimens but rather are casts. The author has not seen any such specimens, but these specimens represent an opportunity to obtain a very early (and usually relatively rare and hence expensive) trilobite at a good price! (Value range F)

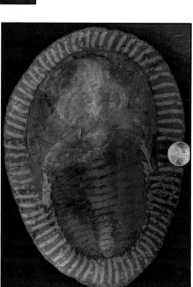

Fig. 09-021. *Cambropallas telesto (Andalusiana)* Djbel Ougrat, Morocco. A superb trilobite obtainable in the late 1990s on the fossil market; specimens sometimes labeled as Middle Cambrian. This trilobite is a unique Lower Cambrian genus representative of the Acadio-baltic or Atlantic Province of the Cambrian. (Value range F, E)

Middle Cambrian Trilobites, North America, or Laurentian Province

Middle Cambrian trilobites come in greater diversity than those of the Lower Cambrian, with new orders and families appearing. Some of these have become well known and widely distributed through the fossil market.

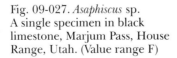

Fig. 09-024. *Elrathia kingi* Walcott, 1924. Group of very common trilobites, often seen at rock shows and rock shops. Wheeler Formation, House Range, Utah. Specimen in upper right has a bite in it, a very early example of predation. The culprit was probably a large, shrimp-like arthropod called *Anomalocaris*. (Value range H for individual specimens, specimens with bite marks are much rarer)

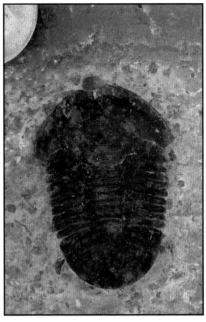

Fig. 09-025. *Asaphiscus wheeleri* Meek, 1873. Another common fossil from the Wheeler shale of the House Range, Utah. This trilobite is next in abundance after *Elrathia kingi* from the House Range. (Value range F, for complete specimens)

Fig. 09-026. *Asaphsicus wheeleri*. A group of two individuals of this genus from the Wheeler Shale, House Range, Utah. (Value range E)

Fig. 09-027. *Asaphiscus* sp. A single specimen in black limestone, Marjum Pass, House Range, Utah. (Value range F)

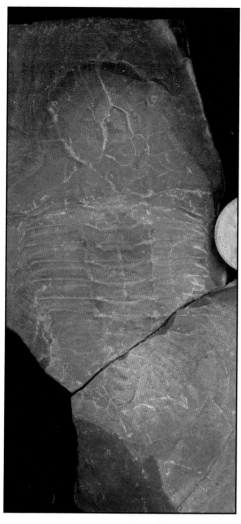

Fig. 09-028. *Hemirhoden ampligye*. A relatively large trilobite from the House Range, Utah. Marjum Formation. Less commonly seen than *Asaphicus* or *Elrathia*, a number of specimens have been obtained from the limy shales of the Marjum Formation. (Value range F)

Fig. 09-030. *Bathyuriscus* (*Orria*) sp. Specimen in limestone of the Marjum Formation rather than shale, which is the usual preservational material of House Range, Middle Cambrian fossils.

Fig. 09-031. Cast of "reconstruction" of *Hemirhoden* with the depth of the original animal not seen on flattened specimens in shale. Such casts have been distributed among collectors. (Value range G)

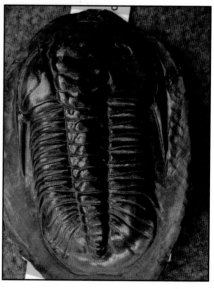

Fig. 09-029. *Bathyuriscus fimbriatus*. This specimen is missing the librigena (free cheeks), a common occurrence with trilobites. These specimens are very flattened on the slaty shales of the Marjum Formation, House Range, Utah (Value range F)

Fig. 09-032. *Olenoides nevadensis*. Marjum Formation, House Range, Millard Co., Utah. This specimen is missing its head or cephalon. Specimens missing the cephalon such as this are molts. The trilobite, like other arthropods, would periodically shed its exoskeleton and then produce a larger one to accommodate its growing body. The molting process involved the cephalon separating from the rest of the exoskeleton with the "head" usually being found nearby. A "free cheek" or librigena is to the right. This specimen is in a hard, black limestone rather than in the softer shale most frequently seen preserving trilobites from the House Range. (Value range E)

Fig. 09-033. *Olenoides nevadensis.* The original specimen from black limestones of the Marjum Formation is in the collections and displays of a fossil museum at Vernal Utah, associated with the fossil exhibits of Dinosaur National Monument. Casts of this specimen are fairly common and have been widely distributed. This is otherwise a fairly uncommon trilobite. (Value range H, as cast)

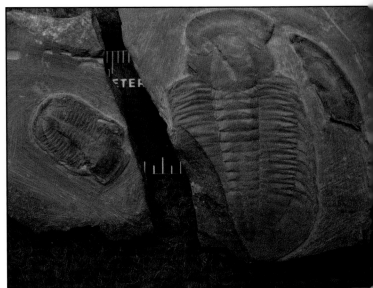

Fig. 09-035. *Glossopleura* cf. *producta.* A widespread trilobite in the Middle Cambrian of the North American faunal province. Specimens of this trilobite have been distributed with labels showing them to be from Manhattan, Kansas. This is not possible, as there are no Cambrian age rock outcroppings on the surface of Kansas. These come from Manhattan, Montana in a geologically complex area northwest of Bozeman. Wolsey shale, Manhattan, Montana. (Value range E)

Fig. 09-034. *Olenoides* sp. Cast of a reconstruction of this distinctive Middle Cambrian genus. These casts, like the casts of an actual specimen, have been widely distributed through trilobite collectors. (Value range H)

Fig. 09-036. *Perioura typicalis.* Marjum Formation, House Range, Millard Co., Utah. A particularly nice and complete specimen of this relatively small trilobite. These are often found in red shales of the Marjum Formation in the Drum Mts., as well as in the main part of the House Range. (Value range E)

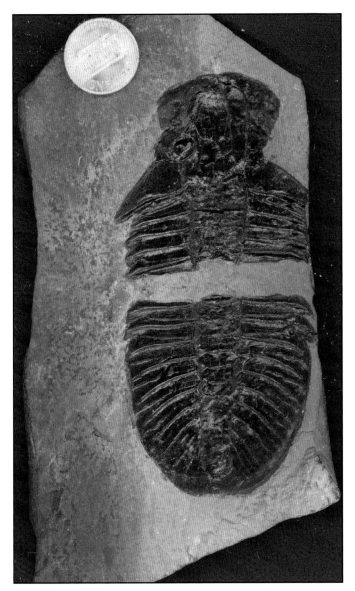

Fig. 09-038. *Ogygopsis klotzi*. Mt. Stephen Formation. Metamorphosed, slaty strata in the vicinity of Metaline Falls, Washington yield a trilobite fauna similar to that found on Mt. Stephen, British Columbia. The trilobites here have been deformed by metamorphism of the shales into slate.

Fig. 09-039. *Albertella* sp. Chishom Shale, Half Moon Mine, Pioche, Nevada. A spiny and ornate trilobite from the lower part of the Middle Cambrian. Specimen is partially disarticulated and is an impression.

Fig. 09-037. *Ogygopsis klotzi* Walcott. Mt. Stephen Formation, Field, British Columbia. A distinctive Middle Cambrian trilobite common on the talus of Mt. Stephen, now in Yoho National Park, Canada. Before this became a national park, numerous specimens of this trilobite were collected by hikers from this talus. The abundance of these trilobites on Mt. Stephen is what gave C. D. Walcott the idea to search for other fossil bearing layers in the area. In 1909, Walcott discovered the Burgess Shale on nearby Mt. Wapta. The Burgess Shale preserves the soft bodied animals of the Cambrian; it's a "window" on the Cambrian Period that lacks the bias associated with most Cambrian fossil occurrences, a bias strongly directed toward animals with hard parts. (Value range D)

Fig. 09-040. *Bathyuriscus formosus* Deiss. Meagher Formation, Manhattan, Montana. A fairly widespread Middle Cambrian trilobite of the North American faunal province of western N. America. (Value range F for individual specimens)

Fig. 09-041. *Kootenia* sp. Numerous pygidia from limestone lenses of the Meagher Formation of the Big Belt Mts., Montana. Such trilobite-rich thin limestone beds represent molts washed into small, shallow depressions on the sea floor.

Fig. 09-043. *Cruziana* sp. Gros Ventre Formation, Big Horn Mts., Wyoming. These are the sediment fillings (casts) of trilobito-morphs (trilobite-like animals without an exoskeleton). They can be quite abundant locally as trace fossils in Cambrian strata. (Value range G for individual specimens)

Fig. 09-042. *Elrathia kingi (Meek)*. This is the same trilobite so common in the Wheeler Shale of Utah. In a down-drop fault block at the east end of Pend Orelle Lake in northern Idaho oc-cur strata bearing trilobites similar to those of the House Range in Utah. This is a group of small specimens from strata that was originally mapped as late Precambrian until these trilobites were found. (Value range H for single specimen)

Fig. 09-044. These trace fossils, which are natural casts, are known as resting pits of either trilobites or soft bodied trilobitomorphs made in mud on the sea floor. A covering of the pits and the filling of them by sand created these sandstone casts. Two large specimens of *Cruziana* from the Middle Cambrian of the Big Horn Mountains, Wyoming. (Value range G for individual specimens)

Fig. 09-045. *Peronopsis interstricta* White, Wheeler Formation, An-telope Springs, Utah. These small peculiar trilobites (agnostids) are eyeless and are characteristic of the Middle Cambrian. They belong to a trilobite order called the agnostida. The agnostids are called that because it is difficult to tell what end is the front (anterior) and what is the back (posterior); they seem to go both ways. (Value range H for individual specimens)

Fig. 09-046. *Ptychagnostus* sp. Another agnostid trilobite. Pend Oreille Formation, Pend Oreille graben, Sandpoint, Idaho.

Fig. 09-048. *Elrathiella buttsi* Resser (right); *Blania gregaria* Resser (left) Coosa shales, Conasauga Formation, Coosa River. Specimens can be locally common in the black shales of the Coosa. (Value range, single specimen H or G depending upon preservation)

Fig. 09-047. *Asaphiscus* (*Blainia*) sp. Coosa shale, Coosa River, Alabama. Deformed shales, similar to the shales of the House Range of Utah, crop out along the Coosa River in northern Alabama and northwest Georgia. These shales contain siliceous nodules, on the surface of which, can sometimes be found well preserved, Middle Cambrian fossils.

Fig. 09-049. Group of large *Elrathiella buttsi* Resser from the Coosa River (now Weiss Reservoir). The species name is for Charles Butts, an early twentieth century geologist who did extensive work in the southern Appalachians of Georgia and Alabama. (Value range F)

Fig. 09-050. *Elrathiella buttsi* Resser. Complete specimen with free cheeks, which are often missing. Specimen preserved in talceous (talc bearing) slate, Conasauga Formation, Chatsworth Georgia, Conasauga River.

Fig. 09-052. Nice, large *Elrathina* sp. (part and counterpart) from near Center, Alabama on the Coosa River. Beside the trilobites, Center, Alabama was the source for a stack of thick Edison Diamond Disk records at a jumble shop. One of these was appropriately, "Down where the Coosa River Flows" (Edison Record #18024), by Vernon Dalhart, an early (1920s) country and western (hillbilly) artist. (Value range F)

Fig. 09-051. *Elrathiella buttsi* Resser. Two specimens on a shale slab from outcrops on the Coosa River near the (now defunct) town of Elrath, Alabama. Elrath, Alabama is the namesake for *Elrathiella* and related Cambrian trilobites like *Elrathia*, so well known from Utah.

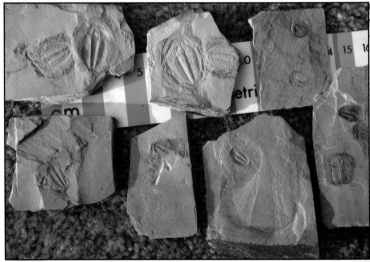

Fig. 09-053. Another group of *Elrathiella buttsi* from slaty shale bluffs along the Coosa River below Rome, Georgia.

Fig. 09-054. *Elrathiella buttsi* Resser, 1927. Coosa shale. Specimen preserved in three dimensions on surface of one of the Coosa River nodules. Coosa River near Coosa, Georgia. (Value range F or E depending upon condition of preservation)

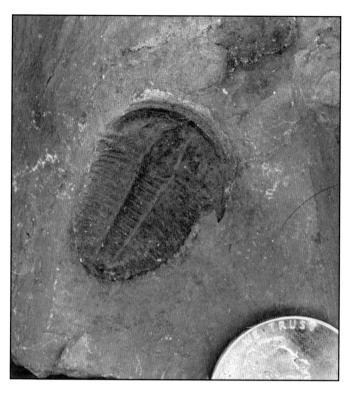

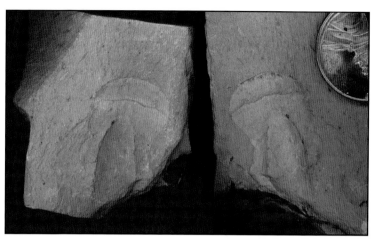

Fig. 09-057. Cephalon (part and counterpart) of a trilobite preserved in slate and deformed from tectonic forces associated with the formation of the Appalachian Mountains. Conasauga Formation, Conasauga Formation, Chatsworth, Georgia.

Fig. 09-055. *Elrathiella* sp. Conasauga Formation. Slightly deformed specimen preserved in slaty shale that crops-out along the Conasauga River near Chatsworth, Georgia.

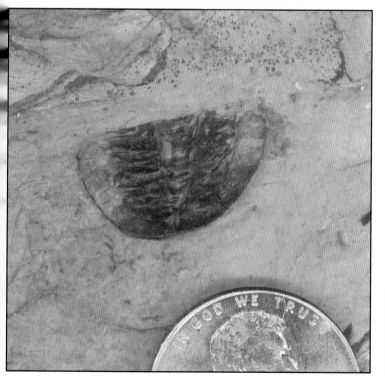

Fig. 09-056. Pygidia (tail) of trilobite preserved in epidote. Highly deformed and metamorphosed strata of the Middle Cambrian Conasauga Formation yielded this fossil, which has been replaced in epidote, a green calcium silicate mineral. The occurrence of this green mineral in the "preservation" of *Eozoon canadense* was pointed out by nineteenth century paleontologists who were proponents of its organic origin. They mentioned epidote replaced fossils like this trilobite tail to skeptics, who doubted the association of this and related silicate minerals with the preservation of fossils.

Fig. 09-058. *Alokistocare americanum* (Walcott). Specimens of this elongate trilobite genus from outcrops along the Coosa River, near Center, Alabama.

Fig. 09-059. *Modochia* sp. Coosa (Conasauga) shale, Coosa River near Center, Alabama.

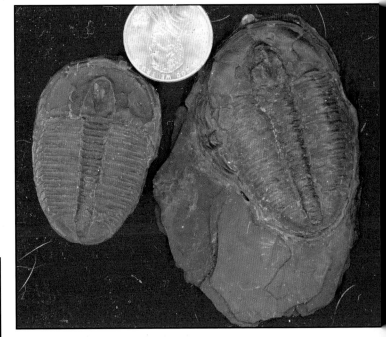

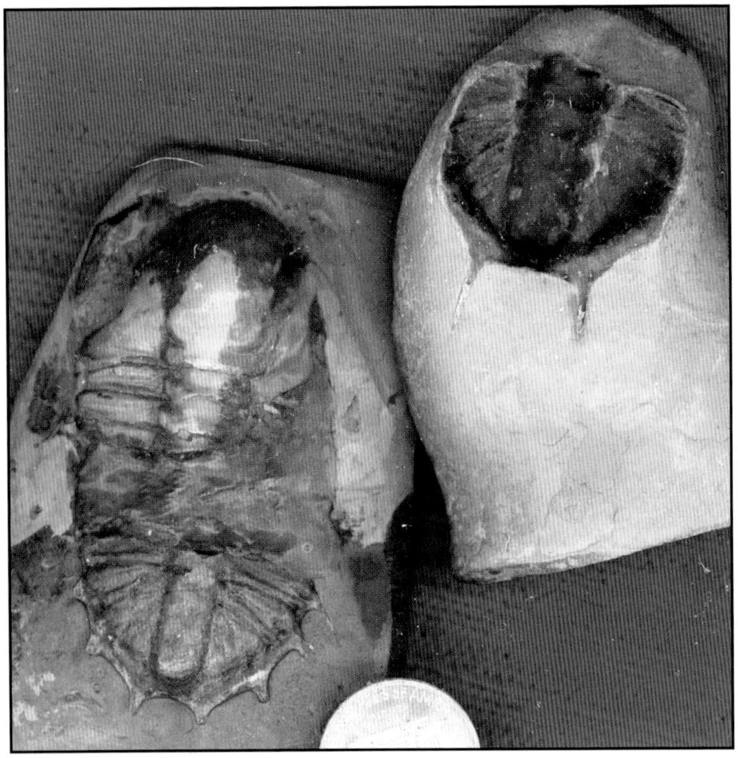

Fig. 09-060. *Olenoides curticei Walcott.* Partially restored specimen in nodule Coosa shale, Coosa River, Alabama. (Value range F)

Fig. 09-061. *Olenoides* sp. Bonneterre Formation (Middle Cambrian portion), Missouri Ozarks. A middle Cambrian trilobite found in lower beds of what are (were) generally considered to be Upper Cambrian strata.

Trilobites from Cambrian Provinces Other Than the North American and Atlantic Province

Fig. 09-063. *Xystridura sant-smithi* (Chapman). Beetle Creek Formation, Mt. Isa, Queensland, Australia. A trilobite that has appeared on the fossil market in the past. (Value range F)

Fig. 09-062. *Damesella paronai*. Lower Middle Cambrian. Yongxun Co., Hunan Province, China. A trilobite that has appeared on the "fossil market" in some quantity, sometimes labeled as being lower Cambrian in age. (Value range F)

Middle Cambrian Trilobites of the Atlantic or Avalonian Province

A number of distinct faunal provinces exist for Cambrian fossils. The North American or Laurentian Province is one; another, with very different trilobites, is the Atlantic Province (also called the Avalonian or Baltic Province). Such provinces represent seas in different parts of the earth during the Cambrian Period—seas that were separated from each other by land masses; land masses that were different from the continents of today. This was part of pre-Pangea paleogeography.

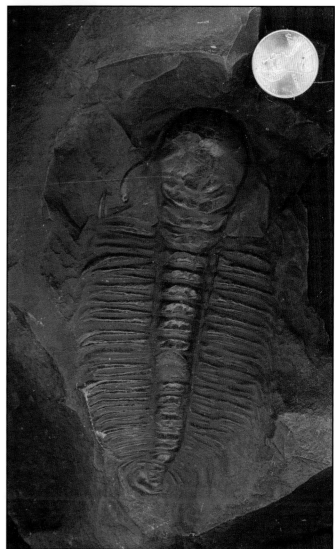

Fig. 09-064. *Hydrocephalus careens* Barrande, Jince, Bohemia. A large number of fine, complete trilobites occur in siltstone outcrops near the small town of Jince, Bohemia, near Prague in the Czech Republic. These brought attention in the nineteenth century as the fauna was discovered early in the history of paleontology and was considered to be one of the earliest occurrences of animals. Its relationship with Cambrian trilobite bearing strata in Wales and North America was unclear, as the Bohemian trilobites differ so much from those of other areas. The significance and reason for these two distinct Middle Cambrian faunas—the North American (which also occurs in western Europe) and this fauna, the Atlantic, Acado-Baltic or Avalonian fauna—was not totally understood until the advent of plate tectonics in the late 1960s. (Value range D)

Fig. 09-065. *Paradoxides gracilis* Boeck, Jince, Bohemia. A large trilobite characteristic of the Atlantic or Acado-Baltic fauna. These are some of the largest trilobites to have lived and can be relatively common in hard, black silty shale. (Value range E)

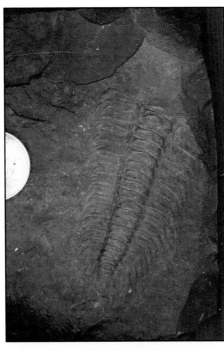

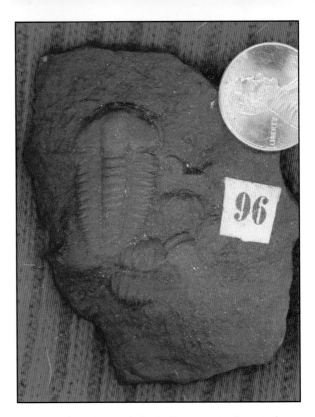

Fig. 09-067. *Ellipsocephalus hoffi*, Etage C, Jintz, Bohemia (specimen bearing the label (96) of F. Krantz, an early twentieth century German dealer in European fossils). (Value range H)

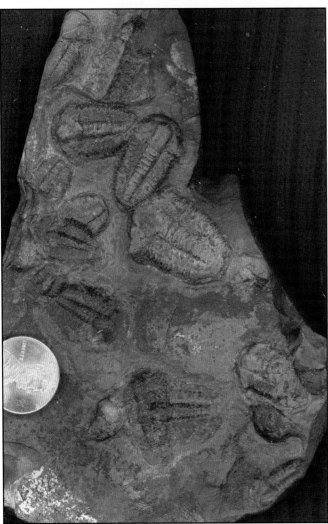

Fig. 09-066. *Ellipsocephalus hoffi*, Etage C, Jintz, Bohemia. A relatively small trilobite characteristic of the Atlantic or Acado-Baltic Cambrian faunal province. (Value range F)

Fig. 09-068. *Ellipsocephalus* cf. *hoffi* Middle Cambrian, Atlas Mts., Morocco. The Middle Cambrian fossils of the Atlas Mountains of Morocco are very similar to those found in the Czech Republic, Newfoundland, and the eastern United States. All of these are preserved in silty sediments that were once on the bottom of the Iapatus Ocean—an ocean that predated Pangea, which split and opened in the Mesozoic Era to form the Atlantic Ocean. (Value range G, single specimen, E for group on slab)

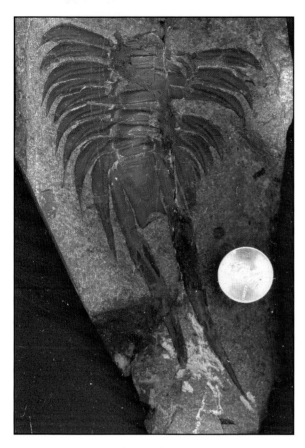

Fig. 09-069. *Paradoxides davidis*, Salter Manuels Formation, Manuels Brook, Newfoundland (specimen missing cephalon). Two long spines extending from this trilobite's pygidium characterize this species of the genus *Paradoxides*.

Fig. 09-071. *Sao hirsute*, Manuels Formation, Manuels Brook, Newfoundland. A relatively small trilobite found also in the Czech Republic.

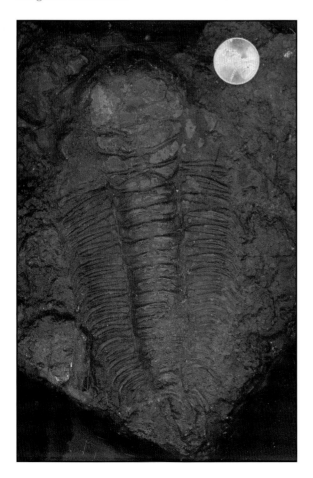

Fig. 09-072. *Acadoparadoxides briareus*, Sidi Abdallah ben al Hadj, Morocco. One of the largest trilobites. These huge trilobites are characteristic of Atlantic Province faunas. Specimens from Morocco offer an opportunity to obtain one of these large trilobites at a fraction of the price of what they usually go for if they would be available in the United States. (Value range D)

Fig. 09-070. *Paradoxides davidis*, Manuels Formation, Manuels Brook, Newfoundland. A large and characteristic trilobite of the Atlantic Cambrian Province.

Fig. 09-073. *Acadoparadoxides briareus.* Specimen repaired, reconstruction evident. (Value range E)

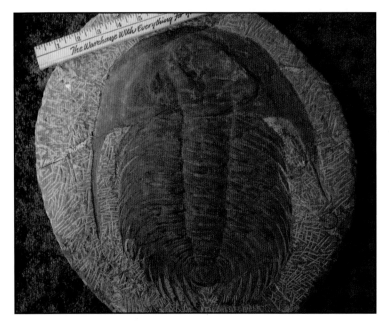

Fig. 09-074. *Acadoparadoxides briareus.* These are some of the largest trilobites known, and an anomaly since in such early strata, Cambrian trilobites are usually relatively small. (Value range C)

Upper Cambrian Trilobites

During the last part of the Cambrian Period, the late or Upper Cambrian, shallow seas covered parts of the continents to a maximum. Upper Cambrian trilobites, unlike those of the Lower and Middle Cambrian types, are less frequently found complete. Usually these consist of the middle part of the head called the glabella, and the "tail" or pygidium. Trilobites in Figs. 09-75 to 09-86 are those of the lower third of the Upper Cambrian, also known also as the Dresbachian Stage.

Fig. 09-075. *Norwoodia gracilis* Walcott Single cephalon, Cedar Bluff, Alabama, Nolichucky Formation. The Cedar Bluff locality is now under the waters of Weiss Reservoir. (Value range H)

Fig. 09-076. *Norwoodia gracilis*, Nolichucky Formation, Cedar Bluff, Alabama. (Value range H)

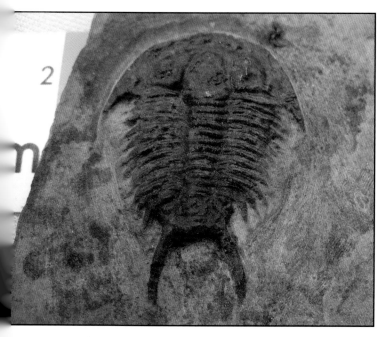

Fig. 09-077. *Tricrepicephalus texanus* (Shumard). A distinctive trilobite with its two spikes on the pygidium. Weeks Formation, Weeks Canyon, House Range, Utah. (Value range E)

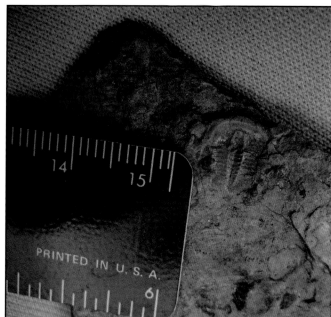

Fig. 09-080. *Cedaria* sp. Bonneterre shale zone (false Davis), Fredericktown, Missouri. Small trilobite specimens like this have low interest for many collectors, although this is a rare locality occurrence. (Value range H)

Fig. 09-078. *Cedaria* cf. *C. prolifica,* Weeks Formation, House Range, Utah. (Value range G)

Fig. 09-081. Glabella of *Cedaria woosteri,* Eu Clair Formation, Sauk Co., Wisconsin. *Courtesy of Gerald Gunderson.* (Value range G)

Fig. 09-079. Group of *Tricrepicephalus* cf. *T. texanus.* Cephalon and pygidia, Bonneterre Formation, St. Francois Co., Missouri. (Value range G)

Fig. 09-082. Cepahlon of *Cedaria woosteri*, Eu Clair Formation, Sauk Co., Wisconsin. (Value range G)

Fig. 09-083. *Coosia* sp. Deadwood Formation, Lead, South Dakota.

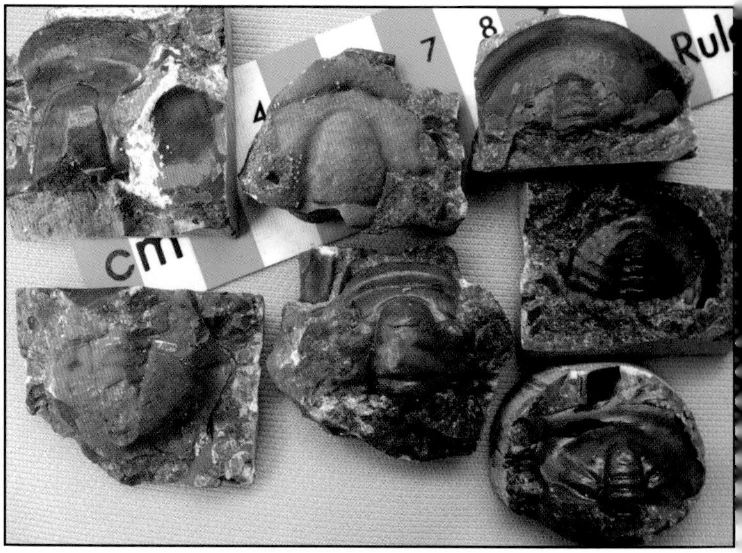

Fig. 09-084. Glabella and pygidia of *Coosia* sp. pygidium to the right and *Tricrepicephalus* sp. (upper middle), Deadwood Formation, Lead, South Dakota.

Fig. 09-085. Cephalon of *Tricrepicephalus* sp. Bonneterre Dolomite, Upper Big River, Missouri. This is how many Cambrian trilobites occur in limestone and dolomite—just the heads (cephalon) and tail (pygidia), although they are preserved in three dimensions, not flattened as they are in many shales. (Value range G for all)

Franconian (Middle Upper Cambrian) Trilobites

These trilobites and trilobite tracks are characteristic of the middle part of the Upper Cambrian.

Fig. 09-086. *Drepanura* sp. A "frilly" Chinese trilobite. *Courtesy of Meng Jisheng, Chinese Academy of Geological Sciences.*

Fig. 09-087. *Cruzania* sp. Trilobite or trilobitomorph tracks or resting pits similar to specimens shown in Fig. 09-43. These may have been made by trilobites or they may have been made by soft bodied trilobitomorphs such as those found in the Burgess shale viz. *Marriella splendens*. (Value range G for group)

Fig. 09-088. Glabella of *Elvinia romeri* (Shumard), Davis Formation, Black, Missouri. (Value range F for group)

Fig. 09-089. Parts of *Housia* sp. and *Elvinia* sp. Davis Formation, Elvins, Missouri. A nice slab of partial trilobites preserved with original material. These Cambrian trilobite slabs are interesting and the trilobites are in three dimensions. Trilobite collectors often pass up some interesting trilobites by not considering such material. (Value range E)

Fig. 09-090. Large glabella of *Elvinia* sp. Elvins, Missouri, the type locality for the genus. These partial trilobites are preserved with original carapace material and are three dimensional. This is a nice specimen. (Value range F)

Fig. 09-091. Glabella of *Idahoia wisconsensis* (Owen) and *Ptychaspis striata* Whitfield. Franconia Formation, Lake City, Wisconsin. Specimens preserved in sandstone. (Value range G)

Fig. 09-092. Glabella and pygidia of *Idahoia* sp. Franconia Formation, Lake City, Wisconsin. (Value range G)

Trilobites of the Upper Part of the Upper Cambrian or the Tempealeauan

In a collection of fossils, the best-preserved specimens are generally the most desirable. Some collectors want only the best and with some groups, such as trilobites, only complete specimens will do. These are the trophy collectors! While very nice, there are only a few of these very spectacular specimens to go around—usually with prices proportional to their rarity and spectacularity. Often, quite good representatives that are not "perfect" specimens go for a lot less. It's the diversity of trilobites that makes them interesting. The trophy collector, by limiting himself to only top specimens, misses out on a lot of interesting specimens, particularly with trilobites as many genera and species are known only from partial specimens. Limiting oneself to only complete specimens limits diversity and that is usually not a good thing.

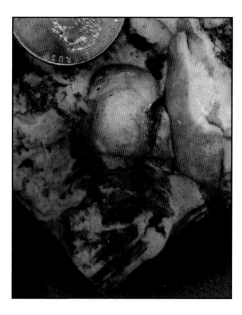

Fig. 09-094. *Plethopeltis buehleri* Ulrich. A genus of trilobite rarely found whole. Eminence Formation, Potosi, Missouri. (Value range F)

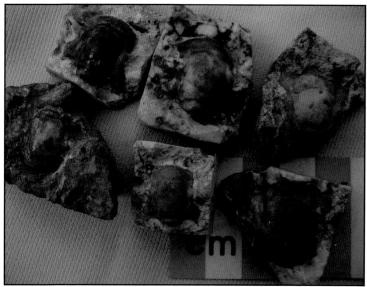

Fig. 09-095. Group of *Plethopeltis* glabella. The usual condition for Upper Cambrian trilobites, the specimens not being complete; however they are often nicely three dimensional. Eminence Formation, Potosi, Missouri. (Value range E for group)

Fig. 09-093. Pygida of broad brim (Saukid) trilobite from southern Missouri. Incomplete trilobites are the norm for most Upper Cambrian strata, however genera like this one are of unusual types. Potosi Formation, Potosi, Missouri. (Value range G)

Fig. 09-096. Specimen of the glabella of *Plethometopus*, another trilobite known mainly from partials, associated with the gastropod-like *Scaevogyra* sp. The spine, which extends back from the glabella, offered protection for the junction between the glabella and the first thoraxial segment of the trilobite. This was a vulnerable part of a trilobite to predators of some type—probably large, soft bodied arthropods. Potosi Formation, Piedmont, Missouri. (Value range E for group)

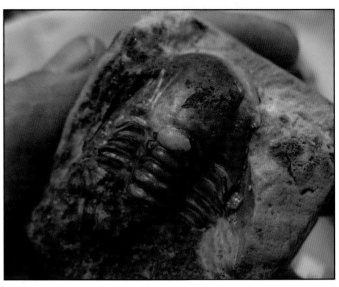

Fig. 09-097. Another partially complete specimen of *Plethopeltis buehleri*, Ulrich, Southwest of Potosi, Missouri. (Value range F)

Fig. 09-098. Nearly complete specimen of *Plethopeltis*. This specimen is a molt rather than an individual that perished on the sea floor The two free cheeks (librigena) to the left were separated from the rest of the exoskeleton when the animal molted. Molting normally produces only carapace fragments. Eminence Formation, Palmer, Missouri. (Value range E)

Fig. 09-099. *Plethometopus modestus* Ulrich. This genus is rare when complete. Eminence Formation. (Value range E)

Fig. 09-100. *Stenopilus latus* Ulrich. A superb, complete specimen of this unusual genus. Specimens of this form are normally known from the rounded glabella. When alive, the animal looked similar to a large pill bug. Eminence Formation, Potosi, Missouri. (Value range D)

Fig. 09-101. Specimen of *Stenopilus* sp. missing cephalon. Eminence Formation, Womack, Missouri. (Value range F)

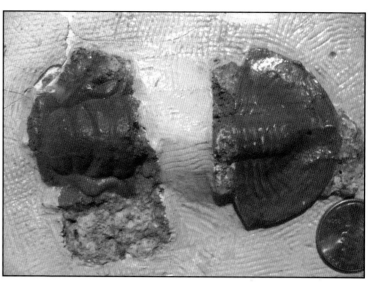

Fig. 09-107. Glabella of *Calvinella* in yellow ocher stained chert (right, red and white chert), formed between stromatolite domes. Eminence Formation, Ironton, Missouri. (Value range G)

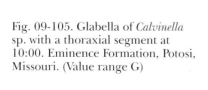

Fig. 09-102. *Entomaspis radiatus* Ulrich. Group of cephalons of this rare genus, which is known only from the Ozarks of Missouri. It is characterized by a broad brim and is a very early Harpid, a trilobite family found mainly in the Ordovician and the Silurian periods of the Paleozoic Era. Eminence Formation, Potosi, Missouri. (Value range E for group)

Fig. 09-105. Glabella of *Calvinella* sp. with a thoraxial segment at 10:00. Eminence Formation, Potosi, Missouri. (Value range G)

Fig. 09-104. *Calvinella ozarkensis* Walcott. This saukid trilobite is known only from the Ozark uplift of Missouri. Shannon County, Missouri (Value range E)

Fig. 09-108. Slab of *Calvinella* exoskeleton parts and fragments of other fossils. Such trilobite "hash" is found associated with granular sediments (packstones), formed between stromatolite domes. Eminence Formation, Ironton, Missouri. (Value range G)

Fig. 09-106. Glabella and pygidia of *Calvinella*. These trilobites are associated with a variety of fossil mollusks that lived associated with and between stromatolite domes in stromatolite "reefs." Eminence Formation, Potosi, Missouri. (Value range F)

Fig. 09-109. Cephalon of *Calvinella* sp. from chert beds north of Potosi, Missouri. (Value range G)

Fig. 09-107. Glabella of *Calvinella* in yellow ocher stained chert (right, red and white chert), formed between stromatolite domes. Eminence Formation, Ironton, Missouri. (Value range G)

Fig. 09-110. Librigena or free cheek of a large *Calvinella* specimen. Seen on the "free cheek" is a radiating pattern of faint ridges, which represent either radiating nerve fibers from the central nervous system or part of an arthropod circulatory system. These fossils are preserved in chert (sedimentary silica), which is capable of preserving fine detail in fossils like these glandular diverticles. Eminence Formation, Ironton, Missouri. (Value range G)

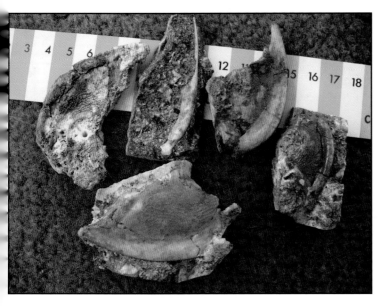

Fig. 09-111. Group of isolated "free cheeks" from *Calvinella*. Potosi, Missouri. (Value range G for group)

Fig. 09-113. Model of complete *Dikelocephalus*. Such models of what this trilobite looked like when complete and not flattened out have been widely distributed through the fossil collecting community. (Value range H)

Fig. 09-112. *Dikelocephalus minnesotensis*. Glabella of a large saukid trilobite found in the upper Mississippi Valley area of Minnesota and Wisconsin. The saukids were large trilobites of the late Cambrian. Lodi Formation, Red Wing, Minnesota. (Value range G)

Fig. 09-114. *Dikelokephalina* sp. A large complete saukid trilobite from the upper Cambrian or Lower Ordovician of Morocco. Like so many Moroccan trilobites, specimens of this otherwise rare genus are found complete in the Atlas Mountains of that country. (Value range C)

Bibliography

Levi-Setti, Riccardo. *Trilobites*. Chicago and London: The University of Chicago Press, 1973.

Moore, Raymond C., ed. "Treatise on Invertebrate Paleontology." Part O, Arthropoda—General Features, Protarthropoda, Euarthropoda—General Features, Trilobitomorpha, 1959.

Chapter Ten
A Cambrian Bestiary (Without Trilobites)

Phylum Porifera (Sponges)

The sponges are placed in their separate, unique Sub-Kingdom of animals, the Parazoa, as they lack organs. All other animals are in the Sub-Kingdom Metazoa and do have organs.

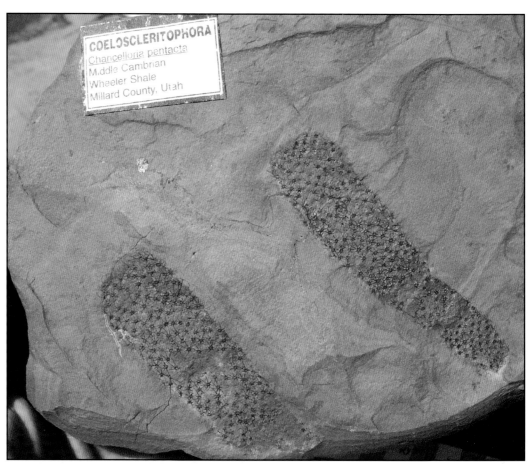

Fig. 10-01. *Chancelloria pentacta.* A complete sponge preserved beautifully in shale of the Middle Cambrian Wheeler Formation of the House Range, Utah. Sponges represent an arrangement of cells different from that found in other invertebrates, an evolutionary "experiment" prior to the Cambrian which led to a body plan different from that which produced the other animal phyla. (Value range E)

Fig. 10-02. Close up of the unique spicules or plates of *Chancelloria*.

Fig. 10-03. *Margaretia* sp. Another type of sponge found in the Wheeler Formation of the House Range, Utah. It is a soft bodied and delicate sponge similar to some of those found in the same age Burgess Shale. (Value range E)

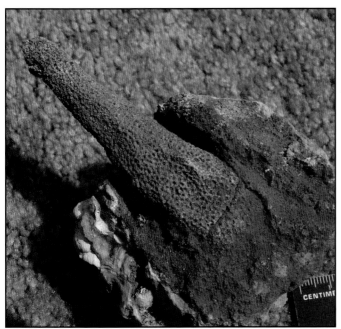

Fig. 10-04. This is a sponge that intermixes with and is associated with digitate stromatolites. Potosi Formation, Washington County, Missouri. (Value range F)

Phylum Archeocyathida (Extinct)

Archeocyathids are considered by some paleontologists to represent an extinct animal phylum. They have attributes of both sponges and corals and went extinct after the Cambrian. There seems to be a lot of organisms in the Cambrian having extinct body plans that are considered by some paleontologists (but not all) as representatives of "experimental" life forms that were ultimately unsuccessful and went extinct before the end of the period.

Fig. 10-05. *Archaeocyathus* sp. A large and complex archeocyathid from the Flinders Range of southeast Australia. Archeocyathids are not sponges since they lack spicules, and anatomically they are more like corals. They are considered by some paleontologists to represent an extinct animal phylum restricted to the Lower Cambrian. Ajax Limestone, Beltana, southeastern Australia.

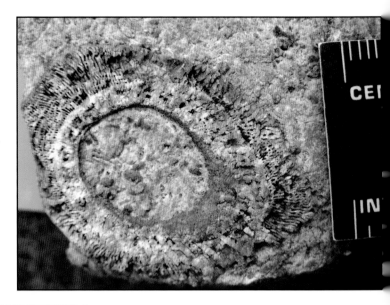

Fig. 10-06. *Cambriocyathus* sp. Archeocyathids are some of the earliest reef forming organisms other than the cyanobacteria, which built the stromatolite reefs.

Fig. 10-07. *Cambriocyathus profundus* (Billings). Reefs of archeocyathids associated with red limestone crop out along the coast of Labrador. These were first discovered in 1835 by Captain Blaylock, a Captain in the British Royal Navy, who considered them to be corals. Captain Blaylock was a close friend of Captain Fitzroy, commander of the *Beagle*, the ship that took Charles Darwin on his famous around the world voyage. In 1865, Elkanen Billings described them as sponges; later work showed they differed from sponges in important ways and also that they were not corals.

Fig. 10-08. *Archeocyathus* sp. Peculiar archeocyathids occur in the southern Appalachians, where they are preserved in barite. This specimen shows the three dimensional conical shaped form of the archeocyathid organism. Archeocyathids are usually seen and studied with polished cut faces or in thin section. Shady Formation, Cartersville, Georgia. (Value range E)

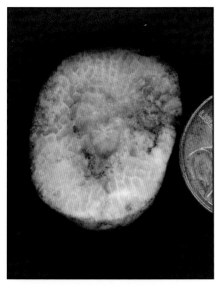

Fig. 10-09. A slice through a Cartersville, Georgia archeocyathid, showing complex structure at the top part of the organism. Shady Formation. (Value range F)

Fig. 10-10. Seascape of a Lower Cambrian seaway with archeocyathids, an olenellid trilobite, and marine algae (seaweeds), by V. M. Stinchcomb.

Phylum Cnidaria, Jellyfish (Medusa)

Jellyfish represent the most primitive members of the Phylum Cnidaria, including corals, sea pens, and the Portuguese man-o-war. Some fossil jellyfish have turned out to be fossils of other phyla and only look like medusa. Cambrian strata have yielded more than their share of fossil "jellyfish."

Fig. 10-11. A collection of fossil "jellyfish" from the Middle Cambrian of northeastern Alabama. In the late nineteenth century, Charles Walcott was encouraged by these specimens to write an extensive monograph on fossil medusa (jellyfish or hydrozoans). The title page of this work is shown here, along with specimens similar to those illustrated in the work. (Value range D)

Fig. 10-12. A colored plate from Walcott's *Fossil Medusa* of the most common "jellyfish" *Brooksella alternata*. This fossil is found in the vicinity of the Coosa River in Alabama and Georgia. Today, Walcott's Coosa River jellyfish are considered to be complex trace fossils preserved in three dimensions in the siliceous concretions that weather out from the slaty shales.

Fig. 10-13. *Brooksella alternata* Walcott, 1898. A group of fossil "jellyfish" from the Coosa River in Alabama and Georgia. Such fossils are known also as "star cobbles." (Value range, individual specimen F or G depending upon size and clarity)

Fig. 10-14. *Brooksella alternate* Walcott. A single Coosa River jellyfish cobble. The large number of these fossils utilized and illustrated by Walcott were said to be have been collected by former slaves in a kind of "make work" project during the Reconstruction period following the Civil War. The Coosa River valley is an extensive cotton growing region, which had large cotton plantations along its banks before the Civil War. (Value range F)

Fig. 10-15. *Dactyloidites asteroides* (Fitch). Slate beds, quarried at the Vermont-New York border, contain a zone of these peculiar fossils. Originally considered to be fossil jellyfish, they are now considered as a type of complex trace fossil. Metawee slate, Middle Granville, New York. (Value range E)

Fig. 10-16. Sandstone slabs containing the impressions of fossil jellyfish from strand deposits. Jellyfish or hydrozoans of today can wash up and become stranded on the beach, drying and leaving distinctive impressions like these. These are from the Mount Simon Sandstone, Middle or Lower Cambrian, Mosinee, Wisconsin. (Value range E, single specimen)

Phylum Cnidaria, Class Anthozoa (Corals)

A coral is like a jellyfish turned upside down and surrounded by a strong, mineralized exoskeleton. Corals are common fossils in younger rocks but are rare in the Cambrian.

Fig. 10-17. One of the earliest corals from strata at the top of the Cambrian of the Ozark Uplift in Missouri. Corals are normally not thought of as being Cambrian fossils, and when they do occur are usually very small. They become common in the middle Ordovician, but before that time, they are rare. Van Buren Formation, Upper Cambrian, Potosi, Missouri. (Value range F)

Phylum Annelida and Other Worm Phyla

Various members of the worm phyla are the makers of most of the "worm tracks" found as fossils. They become abundant fossils in the Cambrian, but are uncommon even in the latest Precambrian rocks.

Fig. 10-18. These distinctive worm tracks or burrows in sandstone are one type of trace fossil that frequently occurs at the beginning of the Cambrian Period. Gunter Sandstone, Camden County, Missouri. (Value range F)

Phylum Agmata and Hyolithids

A number of puzzling fossils occur in Cambrian rocks that have nothing in common with living phyla. Some paleontologists have proposed that these represent extinct animal phyla.

Fig. 10-19. *Salterella* sp. These small, bullet-shaped fossils can locally occur in great abundance at the beginning of the Cambrian Period. They are puzzling as to the phylum they belong to. Some paleontologists suggest that they represent an extinct phylum.

Fig. 10-20. *Hyolithes* sp. Hyolithes are puzzling Cambrian fossils. They are considered by some paleontologists as representatives of an extinct class of mollusks; others place them in their own, extinct phylum. The living animal had a thin shell, shaped like an ice cream cone with a trap door-like cover. Hyolithes are a fairly common Cambrian fossil but are rare after the Cambrian. This is a large Middle Cambrian specimen, Manuels Brook, Newfoundland.

Fig. 10-21. Siliceous nodules or concretions that occur in the vicinity of the Coosa River can contain clusters of hyolithes like these. Preservation of fossils in the concretions is three-dimensional but the same fossil when found in shale is flattened out. Part and counterpart, Conasauga Formation, Coosa River Alabama. (Value range F for pair)

Fig. 10-22. A limestone slab with numerous three-dimensional hyolithes and trilobite fragments. Davis Formation, Elvins, Missouri. (Value range F)

Fig. 10-23. Sandstones of the Upper Cambrian Dresbach Group of Wisconsin can yield nice groups of hyolithes, usually with trilobite fragments. (Value range F)

Fig. 10-24. Quartzites, originally thought to be Cambrian in age (Belt Series), yield these hyolithes. They are from the lower Cambrian as they occur with fragments of the trilobite *Olenellus*. (Value range G)

Phylum Brachiopoda

Brachiopods are shelled marine animals that are not mollusks. Their body plan is more like that of a worm than a mollusk. Brachiopods are common fossils from the Cambrian to the Mesozoic Era.

Fig. 10-25. Frontispiece and plate from *Cambrian Brachiopoda*, 1912 by Charles D. Walcott. A monographic "tour de force" on these primitive animals of the Cambrian; representative Cambrian brachiopod specimens hold down the pages.

Fig. 10-26. Another of the plates from Walcott's *Cambrian Brachiopoda*, with some representative specimens.

Fig. 10-27. Slabs of sandy limestone containing large numbers of inarticulate brachiopods of the genus *Linguella* sp. These specimens come from outcrops along the St. Croix River near Taylors Falls, Minnesota, a major source of nice Cambrian fossils early in the twentieth century. Original, phosphatic shell material is commonly preserved in these early brachiopods.

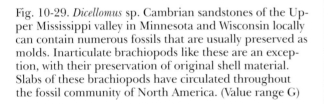

Fig. 10-28. Inarticulate brachiopods from dolomite layers of southern Missouri, similar to those of Fig. 10-27. Subtle differences between these otherwise similar looking shells define genera and species. Davis Formation, Washington County, Missouri. (Value range F)

Fig. 10-29. *Dicellomus* sp. Cambrian sandstones of the Upper Mississippi valley in Minnesota and Wisconsin locally can contain numerous fossils that are usually preserved as molds. Inarticulate brachiopods like these are an exception, with their preservation of original shell material. Slabs of these brachiopods have circulated throughout the fossil community of North America. (Value range G)

Fig. 10-30. *Dicellomus appalachia*. Shale beds formed in shallow lagoons surrounded by hills of Precambrian rocks harbored large numbers of these inarticulate brachiopods in Cambrian seaways that would later become the Ozarks. Bonneterre Formation, Fredericktown, Missouri. (Value range G)

Fig. 10-31. *Obolus lamborni.* Bottommost layers of Paleozoic strata in the Missouri Ozarks contain sandstone beds locally rich in these articulate brachiopods. Lamotte Sandstone, Ste. Francois County, Missouri. (Value range G)

Fig. 10-32. *Eoorthis remnchia.* Articulated brachiopods like these specimens are generally more varied in morphology than are the more primitive, inarticulate forms. This genus is widely distributed in the late Cambrian of North America. It is typical of brachiopods that lived in large numbers in shallow, Paleozoic seaways. Reynolds County, Missouri. (Value range G)

Fig. 10-33. *Syntrophina* sp. Clusters of these small, articulate brachiopods occur in the southern Appalachians as well as in the Ozark Uplift, where these are from. (Value range G)

Phylum Echinodermata, *Camptostroma* sp.

Echinoderms are a phylum of marine animals that are covered with a mosaic of many small plates usually fitting tightly together. Echinoderm fossils are common ones in younger rocks but are less common in Cambrian rocks, where a number of extinct classes do occur.

Fig. 10-34. *Camptostroma* sp. This puzzling fossil is found in lower Cambrian strata of North America. The animal phylum it belongs to is unclear, and some paleontologists have proposed that it represents yet another extinct Cambrian phylum; others suggest that it is an echinoderm.

Phylum Echinodermata, Class Edrioasteroidea

An extinct class of echinoderms that is known only from the Paleozoic Era.

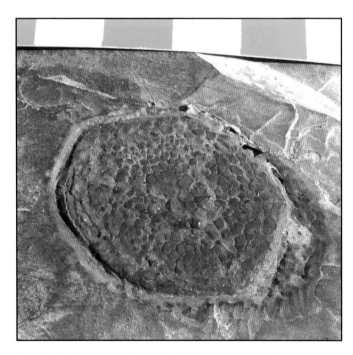

Fig. 10-36. Internal and external molds (part and counterpart) of a small lower Cambrian edrioasteriod. Lower Cambrian, Newfoundland. (Value range E)

Fig. 10-35. *Stromatocystites walcotti* These pentagonally shaped echinoderms belong to an extinct class of echinoderms known as the edrioasteroids. Edrioasteroids are found throughout the Paleozoic Era and these are the earliest known representatives. Some three sided Ediacarian fossils from Australia have been suggested by some paleontologists to be early ancestors of edrioasteroids. These specimens have been preserved in slate that has been deformed by metamorphism. Lower Cambrian, Corner Brook, Newfoundland.

Phylum Echinodermata, Class Eocrinoidea

An extinct echinoderm class primarily known from the Cambrian Period.

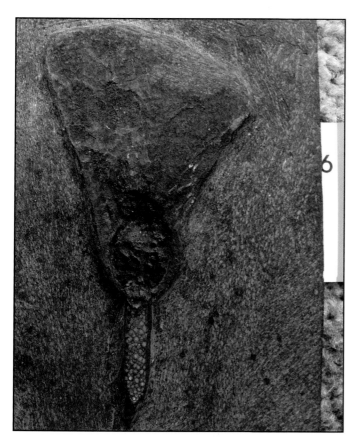

Fig. 10-37. Eocrinoid. This echinoderm, a primitive representative of the stemmed echinoderms, is most common in Cambrian age strata. The lower portion of this plated animal would become the stem of a relative of eocrinoids known as the crinoid. Crinoids are common fossils in post-Cambrian Paleozoic age rocks. Marjum Pass, House Range, Utah. (Value range F)

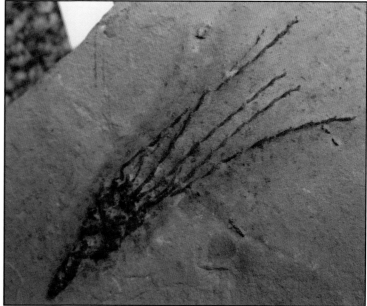

Fig. 10-39. *Gogia kitchnernsis.* A particularly nice eocrinoid from the Spence shale, Antimony Canyon, Northern Utah, a locality that has produced a large number of these extinct and early echinoderms. (Value range E)

Fig. 10-40. Group of typical *Gogia* specimens from the Antimony Canyon locality, Utah. (Value range G for individual specimens)

Fig. 10-38. *Gogia* sp. A small eocrinoid preserved in ferruginous (iron bearing) limestone. Marjum Pass, House Range, Utah. (Value range F)

Phylum Echinodermata, Class Crinoidea

A rare Cambrian crinoid. Crinoids are common fossils after the Cambrian and are still living today; they are also known as sea lilies.

Fig. 10-41. A rare fossil; a Cambrian crinoid. Crinoids are echinoderms that have a stem, which is usually attached to the sea floor. They are common fossils in Ordovician and later rocks but only a few have been found in the Cambrian. Davis Formation, Ste. Francois County, Missouri. (very rare)

Phylum Mollusca, Stenothecoides

A number of puzzling mollusks occur in the Cambrian, including these peculiar fossils called stenothecoides.

Fig. 10-42. *Stenothecoides* sp. Molds and impressions of one of the many puzzling mollusks of the Cambrian. These suggest the shell of clams (pelecypods), however clams do not appear in the geologic record until much later. Another "clam-like" shelled mollusk that occurs in the Cambrian is rostrochonchs; this is a bivalve like a clam, but unlike clams the two valves of rostrochonchs lack a hinge. In *Stenothecoides*, only one valve or shell is present. Many paleontologists regard both Stenothecoidids and rostrochonchs as extinct molluscan classes. Specimens shown here are in quartzite so preservation is not the best. Addy Quartzite, Addy Washington. (Value range G)

Phylum Mollusca, Class Monoplacophora

Fig. 10-43. *Proplina cornutiformis* Ulrich. Monoplacophorans of the genus *Proplina* are single valved mollusks originally considered to have been primitive gastropods. Monoplacophorans differ from snails or gastropods in their segmented soft parts, a feature clarified by living "monoplacs" found in the deep ocean in the early 1950s. Fossils, like these specimens, can show multiple muscle scars on the shell interior, a feature that is indicative of segmentation of the soft bodied animal inside. These, like so many Cambrian mollusks, are internal molds. Uppermost Cambrian, Washington County, Missouri. (Value range G for single specimen)

Fig. 10-44. A group of Proplinid monoplacophorans. The dark specimens on the left are from the type locality in Minnesota where they were first found. These specimens do not show muscle scars like those of Fig. 10-43.

Fig. 10-45. Elongate monoplacophorans of the genus *Hypseloconus*, a genus of monoplacophoran unique to North America. Some paleontologists have placed these elongate monoplacs in their own extinct phylum, the Tergoyma. Potosi Formation, Washington County, Missouri. (Value range G for single specimen)

Fig. 10-46. Mollusks of the Late Cambrian are often associated with stromatolites upon which they fed. This is a group of hypseloconid monoplacophorans along with peculiar gastropods (*Scaevogyra*) in the position in which they were feeding or cropping the algae of digitate stromatolites. The "fingers" of the digitate stromatolites are now represented by vertical holes. Potosi Formation, Washington County, Missouri. (Value range D)

Fig. 10-47. Another view of the same specimen as in Fig. 10-46 but with different lighting. Note the trilobite glabella in the assemblage.

Fig. 10-48. Another pleasing group of Ozark hypseloconid monoplacophorans. Cambrian rocks of the Ozark Uplift can yield a rich diversity of these unique mollusks.

Fig. 10-50. *Gasconadeoconus ponderosa* Stinchcomb. A large kirengillid monoplacophoran which, like most Upper Cambrian monoplacophorans, is associated with stromatolites in a "stromatolite dominated ecosystem." These come from strata that is either at the very top of the Cambrian or at the very bottom of the Ordovician Period. Hypseloconid and kirengellid monoplacophorans are fossils that are typical of the Cambrian Period. Washington County, Missouri Ozarks. (Value range F)

Fig. 10-49. *Kirengella* sp. These hypseloconid monoplacophorans have shorter cone-shaped shells than *Hypseloconus*. Like *Hypseloconus*, they are often found in clusters associated with the stromatolites upon which they fed. (Value range F)

Fig. 10-51. Seascape with kirengellid monoplacophorans and brown algae or "sea weeds." Such a seascape as this would have been seen 500 million years ago between the stromatolites on which a variety of mollusks fed. Artwork by V. M. Stinchcomb.

Fig. 10-52. *Shelbyoceras.* sp. This monoplacophoran was originally considered to be a type of primitive cephalopod. The rounded end had a series of partitions and chambers attached like those seen in a cephalopod shell, but *Shelbyoceras* lacks other cephalopod structures like a siphuncle. This genus and a similar genus, *Knightoconus,* are believed to be the ancestors of cephalopods. Potosi, Missouri, Washington County, Missouri. (Value range F)

Fig. 10-53. A group of shelbyocerid monoplacophorans. These are found associated with stromatolite reefs but are not so concentrated together as is often the case with hypseloconid monoplacophorans. Presumably, they were more active animals than were hypseloconids and would range farther in search of algal salads. Eminence Formation, Washington County, Missouri. (Value range H, single specimen)

Class Mattheva (Extinct)

A number of puzzling, multi-plated mollusks occur in the late Cambrian and are considered by some paleontologists as representing an extinct class or classes. Others consider them as chitons or coat-of-mail shells (the class amphineura).

Fig. 10-54. *Matthevia varibilus* Walcott, 1888. What are collectively referred to as multi-plated mollusks represent more peculiar fossils from the Cambrian, These were first described from the Upper Cambrian of New York state by Charles Walcott. Today, they are considered representatives of an extinct molluscan class (Class Mattheva) by some paleontologists, or to be plates or valves of early chitons by others. Eminence Formation, Madison County, Missouri. (Value range E, for group)

Fig. 10-55. *Matthevia walcotti.* Usually associated with stromatolites, this species of multi-plated mollusk occurs in the Cambrian of Nevada.

Fig. 10-56. *Hemithecella variabilus* and *Robustum nodum*. Two types of multi-plated mollusk, the taxonomic position of which is problematic. Crawford County, Missouri.

Gastropod-like Mollusks

A number of puzzling snail or gastropod-like mollusks occur in Cambrian strata. These are usually associated with and lived and fed on stromatolites. They possess features not characteristic of true gastropods and may be another Cambrian molluscan experiment.

Fig. 10-57. *Pelagiella*? These small snail-like fossils are found at the beginning of the Cambrian as well as later in its strata. They can coil in a right or a left hand direction and, unlike true gastropods, do not exhibit torsion. Eminence Formation, Washington County, Missouri. (Value range H, individual specimen)

Fig. 10-58. *Scaevogyra swezeyi* Whitfield. These snail-like fossils, like all of those found in the Cambrian before the last part of the period, are peculiar. They coil in a counterclockwise direction, while most proper snails coil in a clockwise direction. Potosi Formation, Washington County, Missouri. (Value range G, individual specimen)

Fig. 10-59. *Cloudia buttsi* Knight, 1947. A group of planispiral gastropods belonging to an extinct group of gastropods called the Bellerophonts. Bellerophonts become relatively common fossils in the late Paleozoic where they speciate. This is one of the earliest bellerophontids. Derby Doe-Run Formation, Upper Cambrian, Annapolis, Missouri. (Value range for group F)

Fig. 10-60. The peculiar "gastropod" *Scaevogyra* on the left, next to an undoubted gastropod (proper snail) of the same age. Eminence Formation, Potosi, Missouri,

Fig. 10-61. *Strepsodiscus (Charlostrepsis) paucivoluta* (Calvin). Another peculiar Cambrian mollusk, this genus being bilaterally symmetrical.

Phylum Mollusca, Class Gastropoda (Snails)

Undoubted gastropods appear at the end of the Cambrian. Earlier in the Cambrian Period, snail-like fossils occur but for various reasons are questioned by some paleontologists as to being bonafide gastropods.

Fig. 10-62. Molluscan assemblage. A group of mollusks fossilized in a layer of packstone (granular sediment formed between stromatolites). On the left is a monoplacophoran, to the right of that are two specimens of the planispiral gastropod *Strepsodiscus*, and above these are two specimens of the undoubted gastropods *Dirachopea* sp.

Fig. 10-63. *Macluritella walcotti* (Howell, 1946). Another peculiar Cambrian gastropod, which, although peculiar, is not questioned as to its gastropod affinity.

Fig. 10-64. *Dirhachopea abrupta* Ulrich and Bridge. This is the earliest fossil snail of which there is no question as to its being a true gastropod. Snail-like fossils earlier than this are all peculiar in various ways and their affinity with true gastropods is questioned. Eminence Formation, Washington County, Missouri.

Fig. 10-65. *Taneospira eminensis* Ulrich and Bridge, 1931. Another un-doubted gastropod from the Upper Cambrian Eminence Formation of Missouri.

Fig. 10-66. A variety of large gastropods occur on this slab of the Gasconade Formation of Missouri. These fossils and the strata in which they are found are transitional between the Cambrian and Ordovician Periods. The gastropods here have a rather modern aspect; related mollusks, like the Kirengellids are typically Cambrian. Washington County, Missouri. (Value range E)

Fig. 10-68. Disjunct gastropods of the latest or uppermost Cambrian, Shannon County, Missouri. (Value range E)

Fig. 10-67. A different view of the same slab as in Fig. 10-66.

Fig. 10-69. A chert slab full of small gastropods that lived interstitial between stromatolites and found in rock strata at the end of the Cambrian Period or at the very beginning of the Ordovician. At the bottom right is a small cephalopod, an organism that would come to dominate the seas of the Paleozoic Era and would evolve in the Mesozoic Era into the squid and octopus. The octopus has a highly developed nervous system and brain. It is an invertebrate but its nervous system is on par with that of many vertebrates. (Value range F)

Phylum Mollusca, Class Cephalopoda

These mollusks are successful in today's oceans and are also one of the most evolutionary advanced invertebrates. The cephalopods include the octopus, squid, and the shelled pearly nautilus.

Fig. 10-70. *Dakeoceras subcurvatum* Ulrich and Foerste, 1931. One of the very first cephalopods to occur in the fossil record. These early cephalopods, like their monoplacophoran ancestors, lived in association with stromatolites on which they fed. Groups of cephalopods like these are found clustered between stromatolite domes. Van Buren Formation, Potosi, Missouri. (Value range F)

Fig. 10-71. Primitive cephalopods (ellesmeroids) swimming in shallow water at the time of the Cambrian-Ordovician boundary. Ellesmeroids are named after Ellesmere Island in the Canadian Arctic, where they were first reported. Artwork by Virginia M. Stinchcomb.

Climactichnites sp., Problematic Molluscan Trace Fossil

Large, slug-like mollusks are believed to have made these peculiar trace fossils, which resemble motorcycle tracks.

Fig. 10-72. *Climactichnites* sp. The "motorcycle track" trace fossil. These peculiar fossil trackways found in Cambrian sandstones have long been puzzling. The maker has been reconstructed as a globular, slug-like mollusk feeding upon algal mats that covered sandy surfaces exposed during low tide. Mt. Simon Formation, Wisconsin. (Value range D)

Phylum Arthropoda, Class Meristromata (Aglaspids)

Arthropods other than trilobites are relatively rare in the Cambrian; aglaspids are one of these.

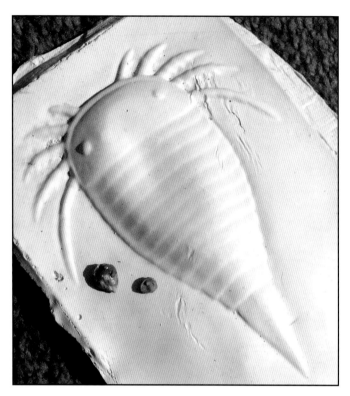

Fig. 10-73. *Strabops thacheri.* This cast of an aglaspid was made from a specimen of this horseshoe-crab-like arthropod found in the Upper Cambrian of Missouri. Two diminutive specimens of aglaspids are to the left of the cast. Aglaspids, horseshoe crab-like arthropods, were not trilobites although they are extinct arthropods. (Value range G for cast, H for small fossil aglaspids)

Fig. 10-75. This trace fossil may be the trackway of an aglaspid rather than a trilobite. Flathead sandstone, Burgess Junction, Wyoming. (Value range G)

Fig. 10-74. A group of fragmentary aglaspids from the Cambrian of the upper Mississippi Valley. Top, head with eyes. To the left of that are small Missouri specimens. Bottom left are two small heads and to the right of those is a rear thoraxial segment. Lodi Formation, Lodi, Wisconsin. (Value range G)

Phylum Chordata, Subphylum Hemichordata, Graptolites

Unknown Phylum

Fig. 10-76. Denderoid graptolite. Graptolites are a type of hemichordate, a subphylum of the vertebrates. Cambrian graptolites were attached to the sea floor; later types were pelagic forms. Dresbach Formation, Afton, Minnesota. (Value range F)

Fig. 10-78. *Tuzoia* sp. Puzzling fossil of a leathery-like organism typical of the Lower and Middle Cambrian Eager Formation, Fort Steele, British Columbia.

Fig. 10-77. A group of Cambrian graptolites from the Dresbach Group, Afton, Minnesota. (Value range F, G for single specimen)

Bibliography

Gould, Stephen J. *Wonderful Life: The Burgess Shale and the Nature of History*. New York and London: W. W. Norton and Co., 1989.

Shimer, Hervey W. and Robert Shrock. *Index Fossils of North America*. John Wiley and Sons and/or Paleontological Society, 1944.

Stinchcomb, Bruce L., and Guy Darrough. "Some Molluscan Problematica from the Upper Cambrian-Lower Ordovician of the Ozark Uplift." *Journal of Paleontology*, Vol. 69, No. 1, 1995, pg. 52-65.

Glossary

Aerobic or oxidizing environment. An environment for life in which electrons are lost and which became common only after free oxygen produced from photosynthesis became commonplace in the atmosphere and dissolved in sea water.

Anaerobic or reducing environment. An environment of life believed to be the most primitive. Some monerans (anaerobic bacteria) can live only in this environment, which is characterized by a total absence of oxygen and other electron acceptors.

Archean. That part of the earth's rock record and the time represented by that record which extends from the oldest earth's rocks to 2.5 billion years ago.

Archeobacteria. A group of monerans distinguished by a genetic distinctiveness (16s-ribosomal RNA) and capable of living under very harsh conditions. The archeobacteria are so distinctive genetically that geneticists consider them to be one of three fundamental categories of life, with the other bacteria and the eukaryotes being the other two groups.

Biogenicity. Something, such as a fossil or a type of sediment, which has been produced by living things at some time in the geologic past.

Biota. A group of organisms that are not animals (fauna) or plants (flora). Biota in the early fossil record refers to a group of monerans or may refer to vendozoans in a context where they are **not** considered to be animals.

BIF (banded iron formation). A type of sedimentary rock characteristic of the early sedimentary rock record that is believed by many geologists and geochemists to have been produced by a chemical reaction of dissolved iron and photosynthetically produced oxygen.

Cambrian. The first period of the Paleozoic Era of geologic time. A time when fossils become relatively abundant and obvious.

Carbonaceous. A material containing a considerable amount of carbon, usually in the form of coal-like material of organic origin.

Chemosynthetic bacteria. Prokaryotes that utilize chemical energy in various chemical compounds as a source of metabolic energy. Some metallic deposits are believed to have been formed by concentrations of monerans oxidizing various ions such as $Cu+1$, $Mn+2$, and $Fe+2$.

Concretion. A hard, roundish body formed by mineral migration in what are usually softer rocks. Sometimes a fossil or other object will form a nucleus around which the concretion formed.

Cyanobacteria. A photosynthetic moneran previously called blue-green algae.

Dubiofossil. A fossil-like structure midway between an undoubted fossil and a pseudofossil. Dubiofossils are disputed among paleontologists as to their being bonafide fossils and hence evidence of a once living organism.

Eukaryote. A cell type that possesses a cell nucleus and reproduces by mitosis; in contrast to a prokaryote, which does not have a cell nucleus.

Erratic. Boulder or cobble foreign to the area where it was found. Usually transported to where it was found by glaciers and then called a glacial erratic.

Ferris and ferric iron. The two oxidization states of the iron atom. Ferric is $Fe+3$ with the loss of three electrons; ferrous is $Fe+2$ with the absence of only two electrons.

Ferruginous. Rock or sediment containing obvious iron compounds or high in iron compounds. Usually brick red or ocher yellow.

Filaments. Thin threads of cell lined end to end. Usually in reference to a type of cell occurrence found in cyanobacteria (blue-green algae).

Greenstone belt. A tectonic setting associated with volcanic island arcs characteristic of the earliest geologic records of the earth, those of the Archean. Greenstone is formed by the metamorphism of basalt when it is buried deep into the earth's crust. Limestone is rare in greenstone belts, partially because during the Archean there was little continental crust, which produces the shallow water, continental shelf where limestone can readily form.

Hadean. That part of geologic time of the earth and solar system that is lacking in the geologic record of the earth. That time before the terrestrial rock record, a time of extensive impact activity from meteorites and asteroids and a time when the earth had a complete or partial magma ocean. The Hadean is presumed to be a time when no life existed on the earth.

Lithification. The process of converting sediment into sedimentary rock. A process that usually involves the passage of some span of geologic time.

Lithology. The general appearance of a rock, which includes the rock's chemical composition, crystal content, and texture.

Megatime. Also known as "deep time" or Geologic time. Time spans that represent the history of the Earth as well as other planets of the solar system, usually measured in tens or hundreds of millions of years or billions of years, and actually measured through radiometric age dating.

Microfossil. A fossil that requires a microscope to observe it. Microfossils can range from just visible to the naked eye down to fossils only 1 micron in diameter,

Megafossil. A fossil readily visible to the naked eye. Magafossils are usually produced by multicelled life forms.

Megascopic. Visible to the naked eye; in contrast to microscopic, which requires assistance (usually with a microscope) to see.

Miller Experiment. An experiment involving a mixture of gases that approximate the earth's early atmosphere, upon which energy is applied in the form of an electrical discharge, radioactivity, etc., the end result being the formation of simple organic molecules showing up in water included as part of the experiment.

Moneran. Single-celled organism that reproduces by mitosis and has no cell nucleus. A kingdom of life in which all members are prokaryotes.

Nebula. A mass of dust, gas, and particulate matter formed from material thrown off by stars and mixed with primordial material (hydrogen) from the Big Bang. Nebula can be seen with a telescope appearing as a mass of glowing gas, often light years across.

Oncolite. A spherical or globular structure, usually 1 cm to 10 cm in diameter, produced by the growth of photosynthetic organisms (generally cyanobacteria) around some sort of a nucleus. Oncolites, unlike stromatolites which are attached to the sea floor, are fee to move around on the sea or lake bottom as a consequence of water movements.

Petroliferous. Containing petroleum. When freshly broken, petroliferous rock will give off a petroleum-like odor (smells like a refinery).

Prokaryote. Cell type that lacks a cell nucleus and reproduces by meiosis. Prokaryotic celled life is represented by the kingdom monera, which was the dominant life for some 80 percent of earth's history. Stromatolites are usually produced by the physiological activities of prokaryotes.

Protista. Single celled organism that has a nucleate cell and reproduces by meiosis.

Radiometric age dating. Method by which a numerical age date can be obtained on geologic material through measuring the amount of a radioactive element decay product compared with the amount of its parent element. The process involves knowing the half life of the parent radioactive element, half life being the time it takes half of a radioactive element to become (or decay) into decay or daughter product.

SNC meteorites. Meteorites of a distinctive type and age believed to have been ejected from the surface of the planet Mars.

Stromatolite. A biogenic structure or trace fossil, generally dome or finger-shaped, which is produced predominantly by the physiological activity of photsynthetic monerans, usually the cyanobacteria.

Trace fossil. A structure in sedimentary rock formed as a consequence of some life activity of a life form that lived in the geologic past. Stromatolites are a type of trace fossil, however the best known and most common trace fossils consist of tracks, trails, and trackways made in sediments that become, over geologic time, sedimentary rock.

Tuff or volcanic tuff. A layered, sedimentary rock made up of fine particulate material (volcanic ash) blown directly from a nearby volcano.

Vendozoans. A group of problematic fossils found in the late Precambrian (Neoproterozoic) and interpreted by different paleontologists as early representatives of modern invertebrate phyla, as an extinct evolutionary experiment in multicelled life, or as fossil marine lichens, as well as other interpretations. Also known as the Ediacarian biota.

Index